'Everything you need to know to prepare you for setting up a business is in this book. Until now, running a business was for those crazy enough to have an idea and take a leap of faith. In this book, Rob Kerr uses project management tools and techniques to plan and execute setting up a business. Devour every word if you want to fast-track success and prevent a lot of mistakes. A practical handbook that will guarantee success.'

Jude Jennison, Leaders by Nature Ltd, executive and team coach, author and speaker

'The journey from employee to business owner is much more than a leap of faith. It's a complete mindset shift. It's like standing on the bank of a fast-flowing river with a desire to reach the other side alongside a fear of being swept downstream.

I know from experience that many won't wade into that river because of the fear of the unknown. For some that's the right decision but for many it is something they will always regret.

Kerr's book *Project Future* bridges that river for aspiring entrepreneurs, empowering them to make the bold decision and take control of their own destiny.'

Rory Prendergast, author and business coach

'I've always had the ambition of starting my own business at some point but never taken the leap or known exactly where to start. This book has helped clarify my thinking, providing well-defined frameworks and clear actionable exercises to make key decisions with confidence and create an executable plan for an exciting future. I would highly recommend it for anyone considering their own venture.'

Bryn Emans

'A must-read for aspiring entrepreneurs. Rob Kerr takes the principles of strategic project management and applies them in a practical, step-by-step process to help you figure out your business sweet spot. Packed full of frameworks, techniques and mindset tools you'll make it happen and make it better.'

Bec Evans, co-founder of Prolifiko, author of *How to Have a Happy Hustle: The Complete Guide to Making Your Ideas Happen* and Business Book Award winner - Startup Inspiration 2020

'The default position of any business is death. It is a risky adventure. Yes, a cheery thought. There are so many moving parts to get right that a wrong decision or move could end in disaster. Having worked with thousands of businesses the main reason is a lack of knowledge and skills of what it takes to run a business.

The FUTURE Method starts to bridge that gap by providing a framework to go through. A risk is only a risk when the odds are against you. What Rob has done is to stack the odds more in the favour of the start-up, giving it every chance to succeed.'

Martin Norbury, bestselling author

'*Project Future* is a really clever mix of structured project management techniques and the skills and attributes needed by an entrepreneur to start and sustain a business. The action steps ask searching questions and if the reader works through them, it will leave them with an excellent plan for taking their business idea forward... or not, depending upon the outcome.'

Lyn Bromley, Managing Director of First Impressions Training and best-selling author of *Trusted*

'An exceptional book that gives you all the frameworks to guide you along your entrepreneurial journey. Full of simple but often easily forgotten advice to ensure you ask yourself the right questions at the right time and, most importantly, take action. If everyone who has done a business goal map with me reads and follows this book, their success for sure will come faster and magnify.'

Kulwinder Dhillon – Helping people set goals and use their own powerful mind, www.kulwinderdhillon.co.uk

'Have you ever thought about setting up on your own as a freelancer or as an independent consultant but got held back by nerves or imposter syndrome? In that case, Rob Kerr's new book *Project Future* is all you need to carry out a thorough self-evaluation as to whether this move would be right for you. This practical and well-structured handbook is packed full of helpful guidance and takes you on a carefully designed journey to consider all that's required for success, from concept to cash-flow. A hugely practical guide, well worth a read for aspiring HR Independents or in fact any other budding business owner or entrepreneur.'

Lucinda Carney, CEO of Actus Software and author of *How to Be a Change Superhero*

'Rob's book provides great insight into the challenges and hurdles of starting your own company – both from an individual and business perspective. Having worked with Rob on numerous different client engagements, we can honestly say that he practises what he preaches. This book will help all budding entrepreneurs prepare themselves mentally for the challenges ahead when thinking about starting their own businesses and entering the brave new world of the self-employed. The biggest attribute that separates success from failure when starting out on your own is self-belief and a can-do attitude – both of which Rob demonstrates every day.'

Mark Bevan & Chris Charlton, Partners at Global PMI Partners, UK

'What a brilliant book! Easy to read and well structured, it makes you really think, and plan, and is a great guide for anyone thinking about starting their own business. I cannot recommend it highly enough.'

Su Britter, HR Executive

Project Future

6 Steps to Success as Your Own Boss

Rob Kerr

First published in Great Britain by Practical Inspiration Publishing, 2021

© Rob Kerr, 2021

The moral rights of the author have been asserted

ISBN   978-1-78860-176-4 (print)
        978-1-78860-175-7 (epub)
        978-1-78860-174-0 (mobi)

For Liên and Wilson.

When the time comes, may your projects be fun, and fulfilling.

Contents

Foreword

If ever a book's time has come, it must be this one. In these post-COVID-19 times, we are anticipating an almighty recession, so traditional businesses are beginning to batten down the hatches. Given how many successful businesses were born out of previous recessions, and that you're now reading this Foreword, I imagine you're exploring starting your own business.

I first met Rob when we were both part of a programme on how to write a book of our own. Having set up my own business in 1994 with nothing but hope, passion and a big dose of courage, I wish I had had the benefit of the wisdom in this book back then.

Rob draws on his personal experience of managing complex integration projects, especially when considering planning and risk – factors often overlooked in the excitement of pursuing a dream.

This invaluable book covers the essentials for anyone serious about setting up their own small business. It's not an 'airbrushed', glossy version of what it's like to be your own boss, but a step-by-step practical guide that throughout asks searching questions of the reader.

He introduces frameworks that will aid you in your decisions, and if that allows some people to realize that setting up a small business is not for them, it will have saved them a lot of financial and emotional pain.

If you're an aspiring business owner, this is a must-read.

I know *Project Future* will give those I coach and train through Flourishing Introverts the confidence to take their first steps by following this robust and considered guide.

Joanna Rawbone, MSc

www.flourishingintroverts.com

Preface

I had a number of false starts in my career. Looking back now, I can see this was mainly due to three reasons.

- I didn't have clarity on my strengths and interests.
- I wasn't willing to make bold decisions.
- I didn't aim anywhere near high enough.

I found the start of my path aged 25, with the insight of others. I'd received feedback during an interview for a finance job that I'd suit project management, but didn't act on it.

A few weeks later, I had a meeting with a recruitment consultant to discuss how they could help me find a role. I took along five CVs covering five specialisms and said I was open to most roles. With the consultant clearly exasperated by this, I was calmly asked to tear up the five CVs, take a step back and think clearly about what I really wanted from my working life.

Then it clicked.

I've worked in project management since 2008 and set up my first business, a project management consultancy, in 2014. Despite warnings that I would 'get stuck offering the same service again and again' and 'never get up the career ladder', my years as a contractor – in dynamic, fast-moving environments full of change and opportunity – were the most progressive of my career in terms of satisfaction, fun, range of experiences, responsibility and the value I delivered to my clients.

I took a step up with each contract and found a niche I enjoyed, helping to deliver mergers and acquisitions (M&A) integration on deals often valued in billions of pounds. I had camaraderie, working in teams of like-minded professionals, rather than the lonely desk in the corner I feared without traditional colleagues to spend the working day with.

My clients valued my simple approach of getting things done, communicating clearly and putting their needs before my own.

But that wasn't enough for me.

I've always taken immense pleasure in seeing other people succeed and find satisfaction. In my career, I've learned that successfully implementing project management techniques can deliver amazing results.

The convergence between those two notions was the spark that became this book, and the accompanying pivot in my business life.

I believe that, given the right preparation, self-employment can be empowering for the individual and can solve meaningful problems in the world. Many of these problems would never justify the investment at a corporate level, and nor could a big business deliver the solution to the same standard as the person who is passionate about making *that* difference.

This book was written to help you prepare to be your own boss, to make the right decision, to make it happen, then, finally, to make it better.

You're unique, as is your journey. For that reason, my approach is both timeless and universal – designed to work regardless of your industry or background.

The role of a project manager is to get the right team in place and bring out the best in that team to deliver the end product. I've applied that principle in this book, so in addition to my own knowledge and experience, where I'm not an authority on a topic I've brought in a contributor who is.

Therefore, this book contains original contributions from 17 people I've interviewed specifically for this purpose. All of them have experience in starting their own businesses, and they cover various fields. Some have shared their knowledge and authority on a certain subject, whilst others have both cautionary and inspirational stories to share about the start-up journey.

They've all taught me valuable lessons, and I hope they add value for you as well. I thank them all for their insight and candour.

You can find out more about the contributors, plus the amazing professional scribbler who drew the unique illustrations featured throughout, in the 'About the contributors' section at the end of the book.

I'd be delighted to hear how the techniques and approach I share in this book benefit you and what better decisions you make as a result. You can join the community in *The Project Future Club* group on Facebook at www.facebook.com/groups/projectfutureclub, send me an email at hello@robkerr.co.uk or discover how we can work together at www.robkerr.co.uk.

Enjoy the journey.

Introduction

The nagging thought

Do you have a nagging thought that just won't go away, telling you it's a fantastic idea to start a business? Whether you've had a desire to become your own boss for a long time, a recent idea, a change in circumstances or a suggestion from others, something has brought you to this crossroads. There is a catalyst for you to consider a change.

For about three years, I had that nagging thought. Then, in 2014, I did something about it. It's been a great journey so far. It's never been smooth; I've overcome many challenges and seized several opportunities that were initially beyond my wildest expectations. You're reading the output of one of those opportunities now.

I love being my own boss, and on my journey I've met many others who feel the same way. If I have any regrets at all, it's that I didn't do it sooner. So, what's it like being your own boss? It's making decisions and being in control of your own future. It's knowing your purpose. It's being confident of your value to others. It's a state of mind. It's being satisfied with your contribution.

Satisfaction comes in many different forms. The most important for me is pride in making a difference. You can make a difference by solving the problems you genuinely care about for the people who, like you, believe that those problems need to be solved. Your own business, crafted in your own image, can be a powerful enabler of positive change.

The aim of this book is not to convince you to become self-employed. On the contrary, if you go through the process and realize it's not for you, that in itself is a successful outcome. You'll have 'scratched the itch' and will be able to move forward without the mental baggage of that nagging thought every time you have a bad day. There is nothing worse than the regret of 'what if?'. And if your circumstances change, you can always revisit the process in the future.

Being your own boss isn't for everybody. It can appear a romantic notion, but it's hard starting and maintaining a business. Nobody will thank you for the lonely hours you put in just to keep the plates spinning. Failure is a real possibility. That's why I've written this book. Before making any significant investment, I believe it's vital to thoroughly think it through and develop a solid base that both you and the key people in your life are signed up to.

Starting a business and getting it right can be highly rewarding. It can change your perception of what even qualifies as 'work'. If you have an idea that would tick enough boxes to justify starting a business, failure to start is the risk.

I hope the tools and methods you'll discover in this book will give you the confidence to make the right decision, make it happen, delight your customers and delight yourself. Perhaps that nagging thought was there for a reason, after all.

What you'll discover

This book empowers aspiring entrepreneurs, freelancers and contractors to ask themselves the right questions, at the right time, to give them the best chance of getting their independent career off the ground – and making it a success. By following my approach, 'that' person could be you.

Leaning on my experience delivering strategic projects since 2008, I show you how to apply key project management techniques just like big business does. You'll discover:

- how to get your mindset in a place where you can set a goal and make it a reality
- tools to give you confidence that your decisions are appropriate to your own unique skills, interests and circumstances
- how to make a plan that focuses on delivering your priorities
- how to take on and manage the right level of risk for you
- how to review your progress and take steps to expand to the next level

Getting the right answers and making it happen is not easy. Making a poor decision (or deciding not to consider a change) can result in years of unfulfillment, missed opportunities and regret. Equally as important as making changes is knowing when to step back and rethink.

By the end of this book, you'll be in a position to think strategically about your future. You'll be empowered to make sound decisions, to be bold and in control.

Why is this a project?

In all business environments, time, money and resources are scarce. It may not appear that way, with big projects often being ubiquitous across the corporate landscape, but for every approved project there are many that don't progress beyond being a concept.

Any significant change or investment must be pitched via a business case, where stakeholders in appropriate roles within the business analyse the costs and benefits, and make a decision as to whether to proceed. They review the business case, pitched by the person requesting the investment, to get the confidence they are making the right decision.

Over the years, I've seen the parallels in this process to those in everyday life. The more strategic we are and the better our planning is, the better the outcome tends to be. The metrics are different, but the principle is the same: analyse an idea, review the benefits, decide whether it's worth it.

As a project manager by trade, I've learned to apply these principles within my own life and to manage change and risk at a level both I and my wife are comfortable with. The frameworks and method you'll discover in this book have evolved through my own experiences. They work because they are simple, yet each step is vital and builds on the previous one.

It wasn't easy starting a business, and it wasn't easy to create the time and headspace – both mental and financial – to make this book a reality. Indeed, my original idea didn't stand up to scrutiny when I fully evaluated what I was trying to achieve and where I was on my personal journey. It takes time and perseverance to settle on a winning idea, followed by a significant amount of planning and effort in delivery to make it a success. That's why I believe every significant decision you make should be considered an investment, just like in all business environments.

Dividing the project into phases

Significant change doesn't just happen. If not managed capably, it can be overwhelming for all involved. A lack of clear direction and control can so easily lead to failure. Therefore, the project journey we'll go through is divided into the following phases and steps.

Phase 0 is about getting prepared. It's the foundation, unseen by your future customers or partners, that'll allow you to get organized, clear and confident. It's split into two pre-steps.

- Pre-step 1: The SORTED Framework, to get your mindset right for the challenges ahead.
- Pre-step 2: The INPUTS Framework, consisting of factors to consider as you develop your business proposal.

Once you're prepared, your project begins in earnest. You'll find out how to make a project plan that'll focus on delivering your goals. Then, we dive deep into the six steps of the FUTURE Method that'll enable you to develop and deliver your plan. This is split across three distinct phases, each with its own plan and objectives to complete in order to achieve your goals.

Phase 1 is about making the right decision. It consists of the first three steps of the FUTURE Method.

- Step 1: **F**ind something you may be interested in doing.
- Step 2: **U**nderstand why you think it could be the right fit.
- Step 3: **T**rial it to prove or disprove your thinking.

Phase 2 is about making it happen. It covers the fourth and fifth steps of the FUTURE Method.

- Step 4: **U**ndertake the activity, now that you're clear, confident and committed.
- Step 5: **R**eview to check progress against expectations.

Phase 3 is about making it better. It consists of step six of the FUTURE Method.

- Step 6: **E**xpand to the next adventure, taking in all the experiences and lessons from what has come before.

Throughout the book, each topic is followed by an exercise called an action. The actions are designed to dig deeper into your personal circumstances, to help you consider how the scenario applies to you and what follow-up activity would benefit you.

Your competition is improving its products and services (its offering) and is talking to your customers right now, so let's start getting prepared!

Phase 0
Getting prepared

Initiating Phase 0

Phase 0 is the foundation which, just like when building a house, is unseen by most. Putting the work in here will ensure that what you build in your business is both strong and right for you.

Phase 0 consists of two pre-steps, each of which is covered in detail. They are as follows.

- Pre-step 1: The SORTED Framework. This is designed to get your mindset right, to become organized, clear and confident. Getting SORTED should ensure you're mentally ready for the challenge ahead and aware of what is required from you.
- Pre-step 2: The INPUTS Framework. This introduces the factors to keep in mind, from both business and personal perspectives, as you develop a proposal for your business in the form of a business case document during Phase 1.

When you've completed the actions in Phase 0, you'll be clear on your mindset and the factors to consider as you find, understand and trial your ideas for a business.

Let's start getting your mindset organized, clear and confident!

Pre-step 1:
The SORTED Framework

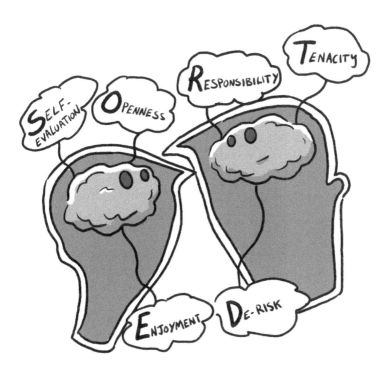

Being organized, clear and confident

When I first considered starting my own business, for about two years I read business books about entrepreneurship. Although I understood the concepts, it was a challenge to picture myself in that position or to work out how I would ever get there. Aside from my skills, experience or business planning, I had to get my mindset in a place where I was organized, clear and confident about what I was looking to achieve and how I was going to do it.

There can be a fear that you may break everything you've worked so hard to build in your career. That's logical. But you'll need to be willing to take managed risks and make yourself uncomfortable in order to make it happen.

This pre-step is about getting your mindset right to run your own business. We'll look into this via the six aspects that form my SORTED Framework.

Be under no illusions – the mindset of a business owner is completely different from that of an employee. As I said in the Introduction, it certainly isn't for everyone. You may get to the end of this pre-step and realize it's not for you. Or, you may get to the end of it feeling energized and ready to take on the challenges ahead.

Mindset change rarely happens overnight. For me, it didn't genuinely occur until at least a year after I had started my business, and I wish it had come sooner. It may click for you at a different time, but each aspect of this framework will benefit you in isolation and as a whole.

At a summary level, the SORTED Framework consists of:

- **S**elf-evaluation: of your most recent role, working legacy, and skill set
- **O**penness to change: opportunities missed or declined previously; being ready and willing to grasp an opportunity
- **R**esponsibility: not being held back by limiting beliefs due to internal or external factors
- **T**enacity: opening doors, being solution-oriented and not giving up
- **E**njoyment: seeing work positively and being energized by it
- **D**e-risk it: being ready to understand and mitigate challenges

Before moving on from this pre-step, we also consider deadlines, making headspace, recognizing your own value and confidence.

Put simply, it's all about you.

Self-evaluation

The only place to start is with a self-evaluation of your most recent role and skill set.

Action 0A

Taking the emotion out of it, ask yourself the following.

- *What is your current/most recent job?*
- *What do you like best about the role?*
- *How long have you been/were you in the role?*
- *What don't you like about the role?*
- *How has the role evolved over time?*
- *Have you driven the change in position, or have you been driven by the needs of your employer?*
- *What does your employer think about you?*
- *How has your career evolved over the last five or even ten years?*
- *How do you feel about the direction of your career?*
- *How have the careers of peers who joined around the same time as you evolved?*
- *What is driving you to consider a change?*
- *What has held you back previously?*
- *What has changed now?*
- *What skill set do you have?*
- *Is your skill set up-to-date and growing in demand, or largely obsolete with a declining demand?*
- *How much investment have you put into training and keeping up-to-date?*
- *How transferable are your skills to becoming your own boss?*

There are many questions here, and each one may reveal something about yourself you hadn't previously considered (or had tried to deny). Taking the time to reflect on your answers to these questions will allow you to think about how and why you've got to where you are today.

Don't worry if the answers aren't as positive as you'd hoped. Accepting your current position is part of the foundation to understanding what you need to change to successfully move forward. Everyone's starting point is different.

Openness to change

You may have a desire to be your own boss, and even an excellent idea. But so do many other people, and many never do it. What can make you stand out is your willingness to do something about it.

Action 0B

Ask yourself the following to assess how open you are to change, and think about how you can improve.

- *What did your self-evaluation exercise tell you about yourself?*
- *How open to change have you been in the past?*
- *Have you perhaps been too open to change, with a lack of structure in your decisions?*
- *Have you actively looked for change or has change found you?*
- *In your career, when a significant organizational change has come, have you seen this as an opportunity or a threat?*
- *Do you fear the prospect of waking up in the morning and not being tied to a permanent job?*
- *Do you have 'imposter syndrome', where you feel you won't fit in or don't have what it takes to succeed?*
- *What opportunities have you missed or declined previously due to being unwilling to change?*
- *How ready and willing do you feel now to grasp an opportunity?*
- *How can you make the most of every opportunity?*

By choosing to do something, including 'no change', you're choosing by default not to do something else. As a result, you miss out on the potential gain from that activity. This is called opportunity cost.[1]

Looking at this slightly differently, it may be that you have ignored the alternative opportunities available to you (or at least not researched

---

[1] Oxford Reference entry for 'opportunity cost'. Oxford University Press, 2020. www.oxfordreference.com/view/10.1093/oi/authority. 20110810105528518.

them thoroughly and considered them objectively) and continued on the course you were on. You may even have been steered onto a new course by your employer to suit their requirements. These are what I call 'tacit decisions'.

Recognizing where you've made a tacit decision in the past will help you avoid making one in the future. The better alternative is to make decisions consciously, to ensure you optimize opportunities that come your way.

Being open to change in this scenario is also being open to becoming your own manager – from initially taking the mental leap to decide to start your business then owning every aspect of it, including the sales pipeline, technical factors, administration and finances. It may be that you can outsource some of this work to an extended team of freelancers or other service providers, but much of it you'll need to do yourself – especially in the early days. How open are you to that?

The following is one of my favourite quotes.

> *There is nothing permanent except change.*
>
> Heraclitus, Greek philosopher[2]

Because of this truth, I always try to find the positives of change. Our perception and the media's focus can often be negative, but look closer and there are almost always winners as well as losers when change happens. Being on the front foot, seeking opportunities and being ready and willing to apply the changes you want, rather than adapting to whatever changes come your way, will hold you in good stead going forward.

Responsibility

It's easy to put off making a decision to start your own business due to some factor or another. The fact is there will *always* be a reason to procrastinate or delay indefinitely. There may be a justifiable reason to hold back, and for that you should use your own judgement. If you want it badly enough, though, you have to take personal responsibility to make it happen. If you don't, it never will.

---

[2] BrainyQuote entry for Heraclitus. BrainyMedia Inc., 2020. www.brainyquote.com/quotes/heraclitus_165537.

Reasons to procrastinate or delay fall into two categories – internal factors and external factors.

Internal factors include family responsibilities, waiting for the outputs of a promotion review at work, holding back for a bonus or even the prospect of a redundancy payment that may never come. The prospect of additional start-up capital may be useful, but factor in whether it's absolutely necessary. You may always think you don't have enough time, money or knowledge. Such a delay goes back to the opportunity cost of continuing on the current path and therefore denying yourself the opportunities that may come from your new business. They could be legitimate reasons to think twice, but at the same time, if you genuinely want to get something done and your analysis stands up to scrutiny, you shouldn't let yourself be delayed. In some form or another, these reasons are likely to exist permanently.

External factors include changes to government regulations, a fragile political climate, a weak economy or announcements from competitors that the market is looking downwards. All of these external factors create change, and with change come the conditions for renewal. It may sound counter-intuitive, but if businesses are failing, something will need to take their place. It may be a different solution or way of delivering it, but it's rare for demand to simply evaporate. Such renewal could be *your* opportunity.

Whether the factors are internal or external, these are all examples of limiting beliefs. If a roadblock exists, your mindset as a business owner shouldn't be to accept the situation and be held back, but to work out how to get around it and succeed regardless. You'll need that innate belief that it can be done, and that you can get there.

Action 0C

Take a look at both internal and external factors that may be stopping you moving forward. Consider first if they're genuine blockers. If they are, put a timeline against when you expect the blocker to be overcome. Everybody's personal circumstances are different, so internal factors can be highly complex, but think hard about the validity of external factors. If somebody else is able to overcome them, the chances are you can too.

Tenacity

It's easy to think that those who are successful as their own boss are highly skilled experts at what they do, well qualified and super clever, but those traits in themselves are not enough to guarantee success. If you want to succeed in your venture, you have to be willing to do the hard, uncomfortable work, and put yourself in a position where you can – and do – fail.

It's about the unseen hours of research, crafting your offering and pitch, being rejected and then keeping your chin up, learning lessons, amending your offering and pitch, then risking failure all over again.

You have to see opportunities where they don't appear to exist, constantly solve problems and overcome obstacles. You must have confidence in your business and yourself, and make your argument so compelling that it becomes impossible for the right people to say no. You shouldn't give up when the problem seems to have no solution. Persevere when nobody is paying attention. Stay focused on the task in hand, avoiding all manner of distractions that exist in the twenty-first century from social media, email, 24-hour news and sport. Tenacity is about focusing on delivering an objective, believing in yourself that you can achieve the outcome or goal and having the drive to make it your reality.

There are some tricks to help with this. One is to pick the right goal. If you believe in it, even love it, you're more likely to stick with it and to convince your customers you're the right person to deliver what they need or want. If you don't believe in it, I can almost guarantee your competition will.

If you aren't willing to be tenacious, to back yourself and your business, you may as well stop now.

Action 0D

Look for two to three examples, be they in your personal or professional life, where you have been tenacious, like a dog with a bone, not willing to take 'no' for an answer.

- *How can you channel this determination into the launch of your business?*

Enjoyment

I was once told by a family member that 'work is to be endured, not enjoyed'. My response to this was simple: 'Only if that's what you choose to accept'.

I strongly believe it's possible to enjoy work, and if you don't enjoy what you're doing it's time to look for something new. Even if you do enjoy your work but are not feeling satisfied, it's a sign that your path leads elsewhere.

Although officially cited as of unknown origin, the below quote[3] is sometimes attributed to the Chinese philosopher Confucius,[4] around 2,500 years ago.

> *Choose a job you love, and you will never have to work a day in your life.*

I don't believe work is about earning money to pay the bills and facilitate other things you enjoy. It's a much bigger opportunity than that. It's about solving problems that are important to you, for the people who believe solving these problems is important. It's about the journey rather than the destination, and that journey is what you live every day of your working life.

If you search the internet for job satisfaction or what makes a great job, studies consistently show that money is not the key factor for high morale and motivation. That's not to say money isn't important, but after a threshold of being able to live comfortably, whatever that may mean to you, then it has little impact on job satisfaction. A sense of achievement and the opportunity to be challenged, to learn and to help others are far more prominent reasons people are satisfied with their occupation.

To apply this in what you do requires a subtle mindset shift of not working for money but, rather, money becoming a welcome byproduct of what you choose to do with your time. Looking one step further, most incredibly successful people work when they don't have

---

[3] BrainyQuote entry for unknown author. BrainyMedia Inc., 2020. www. brainyquote.com/quotes/unknown_134717.

[4] See https://quoteinvestigator.com/2014/09/02/job-love/.

to, because they love what they do, have the drive and it's what gets them up in the morning, often into old age.

It's also possible to say that enjoying work has its own financial upside. This is because you may be willing to put more energy into something you enjoy, and therefore deliver things people find valuable and are willing to pay for.

And that's the key point – to be motivated you must enjoy doing it and consider it meaningful. What you do to earn a living then becomes a part of your life, with its own rewards, rather than that negative thing called 'work'.

Work can be draining. I've seen colleagues many times, and have been there myself, completely exhausted by Friday afternoon, then just about recover by Monday morning, ready to do it all again. On the other hand, work you consider meaningful can be incredibly energizing. In that situation, Monday mornings are never a chore.

If you can work because you want to, rather than because you have to, it's a positive way to go about your working day and your life.

Action 0E

Draw a line down a page, labelling one column 'Enjoy' and the other 'Endure'. Consider what aspects of work you've done to date you've enjoyed, and what you've endured. How is that balance? There may be no perfect answer and you'll always have to endure some things. Some aspects may even go on both sides of the equation depending on your circumstances at the time – from my experience, working away from home has been in both categories over the years.

- *How can you ensure that you enjoy more and endure less going forward?*

De-risk it

Risk management is fundamental to the success of any project. Risks exist in just about every scenario, and how you respond and manage them will be key to whether you succeed or fail.

People's perception of risk, and appetite for it, varies considerably. You may be particularly risk-averse, with a high perception of risk and low appetite for it, in which case you'll need significant proof that a change or investment is justified.

At the other end of the spectrum, your perception of risk may be low and appetite high, in which case you may settle for too little proof that a change or investment is justified.

Understanding your own perception of and appetite for risk is an excellent starting point. Especially if you're towards either end of the spectrum, strong risk management will ensure you make fact-based decisions, assessing all risks on their own merits.

The first step is to have visibility of what you're looking to achieve and what your risks are. The second step is to size them before deciding when and how you're going to mitigate them.

In the 'Responsibility' sub-step (above), we looked at reasons that could hold you back and being ready to work around them. Accepting that risks will always be there and being prepared to mitigate them is how you achieve this.

Your initial risk reduction could be to start your business as a 'side-hustle', in your spare time alongside your regular income. Or you may choose to run your business from home rather than invest in costly premises, for example.

The opportunity cost of being an employee can also be looked at as a risk to be mitigated. By deciding to work for an employer and conduct a role in return for a salary, you're denying yourself the option to do something else. The longer you're there, the more embedded you are within the company, its culture and ways of working, and therefore the bigger the risk is perceived to be for leaving.

We'll look at managing risk in more detail in Step 2: Understand, but initially when it comes to getting your mindset right, before thinking about finances, products, services, suppliers, customers or competition, the biggest risk you'll need to overcome is yourself and your mentality to default to the role of employee.

Action 0F

Take a bit of paper and write a leading statement, 'As a...', followed by, 'There is a risk that...', and on a line below, 'I will mitigate this by...'. Start a timer for ten minutes and write. You may be surprised by what you come up with.

- *What do the results tell you about your perception and appetite for risk?*
- *How can you make sure the risks you raise are justified?*

There's nothing like a deadline

I've lost count of the number of projects – both professional and personal – I've worked on when all seemed lost, disorganized and doomed to failure. Then it came together at the last minute and turned into such a success that I wondered what all the fuss had been about.

This is down to the power of a deadline. A deadline is a reframing technique that gives the mind clarity, leading to focus, commitment and ultimately productivity to get over the line and deliver on commitments.

I love running. It makes me feel fresh and energized. Yet over the years I've often gone weeks or even months at a time without running at all. When I signed up to run the 2014 London Marathon with a commitment to raise £2,000 for the charity Children with Cancer UK, the need to be ready for that deadline prevented any procrastination I would normally have done and made me prioritize time for training that I would normally have used for something else.

I was terrified of running the London Marathon. Before starting training I'd only ever run a single half-marathon and a few ten-kilometres. A few years beforehand I couldn't even run 200 metres without stopping, out of breath, to hug a lamppost. You could say I was inexperienced for such a challenge.

A deadline helps to programme the brain to make an aspiration so remote or unfeasible feel possible, allowing you to meet your objectives and succeed, as I did on that wonderful day.

Action 0G

Practice setting deadlines in your daily life and see how your productivity increases. The fear of failure needs to be enough to ensure your commitment; otherwise, it's easy to kick the can down the road and nothing will ever get done. Commit to delivering by the deadline and you'll get into the routine of making and meeting deadlines, and as a result will make a strong plan and stick to it.

Making headspace

There are only so many hours in the day, and even with a clear deadline, it can be difficult to make things happen. In order to make time in your day, which I call headspace – quality thinking time – some things will probably need to change.

You could modify your *leisure* time – social or relaxation activities that you could stop, reduce or delay, but this may result in you resenting your business planning. This wouldn't be a good way to start your relationship with your business.

It may be that multi-tasking is a better alternative. Many of the best ideas I had for this book and my business came during my leisure time – normally running or swimming. After a while, I recognized this and therefore didn't feel guilty about spending time for myself; this was legitimate business growth time and the fact I enjoyed it was secondary.

We all have some commitments that are absolutely *essential* and cannot be moved. Therefore, see how you can become more efficient at doing some of the things you don't enjoy but that nonetheless form part of your daily activities. Paying bills, managing the house and car – these are all things that take time and energy and can, to some extent, be simplified.

A few years ago, I'd had enough of the regular tasks that were on my list and decided to put all the bills on direct debit. I opened a new bank account just for this purpose and fulfil that account with a standing order payment from my main account. This has saved me at least an hour every week in real time, but significantly more in headspace time. I'm not constantly thinking about things that need to be done and when thoughts wander I can instead think about something more productive, like developing my business.

Equally, consider what other regular tasks you can reduce or outsource. We'd never had a cleaner – it just wasn't something that was in my background – but getting one and mentally considering it an investment made a big difference to my productivity. Instead of thinking of it as paying someone to sweep and mop for two to three hours each week, I considered it a cost that allowed me to work on my business for two to three hours, when I could add genuine value and create something. It's a subtle change but justified my investment in a cleaner.

Also, consider things like grocery shopping. It takes time, and I still have to physically go to the shops, but as a family we've added online shopping to our routine, which has made trips to the supermarket shorter and less frequent. The time freed to work on the business more than makes up for the investment in the delivery charge.

Finally, you could make better use of your *downtime*. You may not have a lot, but there are windows in the day where you could make small, effective changes to use the time positively towards your proposed business. If you commute, what could you change in your routine to make time for headspace? In the evenings, what distractions, like browsing social media, news and TV, could you reduce or eliminate from your routine? These things often don't add any value but can swallow an alarming amount of time that you could use more productively.

Whatever you decide to change, make a conscious effort to be in control of your time and lead, rather than be led.

Action 0H

Categorize the activities you complete each week as 'leisure', 'essential' or 'downtime'. Make a list of what opportunities there are for you to make time in your week without compromising on what you need to do, or like doing. Look at the cost of the investment, time freed and how quickly it can be implemented before deciding what to prioritize. Consider how you can block time for clear headspace.

- *In what environment do you do your best creative thinking?*

Recognizing your own value

Especially if you've been in one company for a long time, it can be difficult to recognize the value that others see in you and how you can transfer this to a new audience. Instead of looking at *what* you do – in my case, 'Project Manager' – define it by the outputs: the *why*. A former headline I had on LinkedIn was 'Helping senior leaders successfully deliver M&A integration'. And that's the key point: delivery. One way or another, your employer has felt the need to invest in you to deliver something of value.

Now your challenge is to recognize your own value. Invest time, energy and perhaps money in yourself to get clarity on the value you can deliver to others who will become your new customers. Once you've recognized it you'll need to get your offering and pitch clear so others can see your value and why they need it, allowing you to move forward on your own path.

Action 01

Take the job titles you've had over the years and turn each into a sentence of fewer than ten words explaining what value you delivered in the role.

- *What problems did you solve?*
- *What did you deliver?*
- *What did you take ownership of?*
- *What solutions did you develop?*
- *Who did you take a burden from?*
- *How were they then freed to solve other problems?*

Once you recognize what value you've delivered, consider how you can channel the elements you enjoyed going forward.

Taking confidence from yourself

There is a big difference between being confident and being over-confident or complacent. At the other end of the scale, if you're nervous about what awaits you, that's normally positive. Being nervous shouldn't stop you from feeling confident, and if you don't believe in yourself, nobody else will.

Many business owners would never have foreseen themselves being in that position. I never did! But circumstances change, and in order to achieve the satisfaction and balance you want from your business, you must be confident that you can make it happen. You'll need to see failure as an opportunity to learn. You'll need to put yourself out there to be judged by strangers in the big, wide world.

I referenced my achievement in completing the London Marathon in terms of the importance of a deadline, but it's also benefitted me in so many other ways. It's no coincidence I set up my own business eight months after running it. It gave me the confidence that I could commit publicly and complete significant challenges. Retrospectively, it's also something I'm proud to talk about. I stand taller when talking about it, and it shows others I can get stuff done.

Although the long-term goal in that scenario was to run the marathon, there were so many smaller objectives within my training plan that gave me the confidence I could do it. There were bad days, and things I had to amend. I felt like giving up on more than one occasion during training. But by race day, I was ready. I knew I was ready, and all negative thoughts had vanished. I took it to the stage and delivered it.

By reading this book you're taking a positive step to set yourself up for success. There are a lot of difficult questions you'll need to ask yourself and even more hard thinking required to find the right answers. There will be challenges to overcome, and undoubtedly setbacks. However, if you persevere, are honest with yourself, back yourself and take the right feedback on board, there is absolutely no reason you shouldn't be confident and, ultimately, succeed.

Action 0J

Take a step back and look at your achievements to date – in work, in your home life or in a social setting. It's easy to just move on to the next objective and forget about achievements, but taking pride in what you've done and being willing to tell people about it should build your confidence and give you a platform from which to grow.

Retrospective

From this pre-step, you should now be clear on how the SORTED Framework applies to you, and what areas you especially need to focus on. You may be comfortable with how open to change you are, for example, but need to work on your techniques and confidence to be more tenacious.

I cannot overstate the importance of your mindset to the journey ahead. If you believe you can make it happen, you'll find a solution. The opposite is also true.

To receive a personalized report based on this pre-step, go to my website, www.robkerr.co.uk, and complete a quiz in three minutes. The report will outline your strengths and areas for improvement.

Now let's start looking at the factors you should consider, from both business and personal perspectives, as you develop a proposal for your business!

Pre-step 2:
The INPUTS Framework

The business case

In the Introduction, we covered how and why businesses use a business case. Don't confuse this with a business plan, which is a thorough roadmap with goals and financial projections, often used when seeking external investment.

A business case is an internal document to justify the investment of your own time, money and energy. For our purpose in this pre-step, we are looking at what goes into a business case to develop a strategic proposal for your new business.

You're your own board of directors, and you must make the decision of whether to invest in your proposed business in favour of the alternative options. You're in control, and it's very exciting.

Introducing the INPUTS Factors

What's important for your investment is not the same as what's important to big business. I've created the INPUTS Business Case Framework (shortened to INPUTS Framework) so you can critically analyse your proposed business investment before you commit time, money or energy into something that may not be the right path for you.

There are six independent cases, or factors, within the framework that together will form your business case. In order to maximize the quality of your proposal, consider them equally.

As you develop and refine your business case during Phase 1, these six factors should give you clarity and confidence that you're making the right decision.

At a summary level, the INPUTS Framework consists of:

- the **I**mpact factor: recognition of what impact your decision will have on key people in your life
- the **N**umbers factor: an assessment of your personal finances and what your proposed business will require initially, and what it will provide as a return on your investment
- the **P**ersonal factor: to determine whether the project is suitably aligned to your personal characteristics and circumstances
- the **U**seful factor: consideration of what skills you'll need to source externally to support the delivery of your offering
- the **T**iming factor: an appraisal of your own commitments and likely commitments
- the **S**ales factor: a review of the market you propose to go into, and where you fit in

There will be dependencies on some factors to enable others. For example, clarity is needed on what you'll sell, and to whom (from the sales factor) before you can complete your sales forecasting (in the numbers factor). All six factors should, therefore, be cohesive to form a unified business case proposal document.

Don't worry if you cannot complete many of the actions now. The value is being aware that these are questions to be answered. We build on this throughout Phase 1, ahead of completing and signing off your business case at the end of Phase 1.

Let's look at each factor in detail.

The impact factor

Every major decision you make in life has an impact on other people. Whether it's your spouse, children, extended family, friends or a combination of them, someone's role, responsibilities and lifestyle is highly likely to change as you undertake your project and start a business. After our two children were born, my wife Trang decided to start her own jewellery business. For many months the impact on me was quite small, as she largely focused on her work late in the evening, after the children had gone to bed.

In the lead-up to the launch, however, she was working heavy hours during the day, late into the evenings and throughout weekends to get everything prepared. The impact this had on me and the children was significant as routines and responsibilities within the family set-up changed. I also had a full-time client and was often away from home for two to three days per week.

We got through it and made it happen, and then learned from the experience so that when the next big decision came around – me wanting to take time away from client work to write this book – it was a joint decision we both signed up to.

> **Action OK**
>
> *Identify the key people in your life. Consider what impact your decision will have on them and discuss it with them through a worst-case scenario covering effort needed and duration. Understand how you can get those key people onside, and have their support in advance of the undertaking. It could be vital to your success.*

The numbers factor

Whatever it is you decide to do, it's highly likely you'll be looking for a financial return on your investment of time, money and energy. Like many areas, this is split into both personal and business considerations.

Action 0L

Complete a financial assessment, covering your personal circumstances and business planning. Ask yourself the following.

Personal

- *How much do you have in savings?*
- *How much of your savings are you willing to commit?*
- *How much money do you need each month to cover your personal outgoings?*
- *How long will your savings stretch?*
- *Do you need a bank loan or other investment?*
- *If you need it, are you likely to get approval for a bank loan or other investment?*
- *What options do you have if it doesn't go to plan?*
- *How important to you is the highest available financial return?*

Business

- *How long will it take from when you start until you make your first sale?*
- *How much start-up money do you need to invest before you make a sale?*
- *What are your fixed costs, per month?*
- *What are your variable costs, per sale?*
- *What profit mark-up will you look to achieve, per sale?*
- *What does your sales forecast look like from month 1 to month 36?*
- *How long before your initial investment is paid back?*
- *How high is the return on investment (ROI) over a three-year period?*

A key part of the INPUTS Framework is this initial financial assessment and the answers to the questions above also build into the other considerations. For example, there may be a financial impact on your spouse's lifestyle, with less money coming in and/or joint savings being used in your business investment that they'll need to agree to.

In the business world, a financial return is generally the key performance measure when deciding whether to make an investment. Although this is likely to be a measure for you to some extent, there are other factors that come into play.

You'll need to decide what weighting you put on doing something you love that may provide a lower financial return than something you're merely good at, or wouldn't enjoy as much in the day-to-day but may provide a more comfortable financial return or lower risk. This can be in terms of both an alternative project to invest in, or the 'do nothing' option – a continuation on your current path.

The personal factor

Putting others and finances to one side, let's think about you. Only you can decide what you want to do with your day, every day for the foreseeable future, and therefore whatever you decide must be suitably aligned to your individual skills, interests and circumstances.

Action 0M

When analysing your proposal, focus on the following.

- *How do your current knowledge, experience and skills align with what you want to invest in? Are there any gaps that may need to be filled before you start?*
- *How does this business investment link to your interests and hobbies? Do you have a passion for it, to hold your attention?*
- *What's your work ethic and the priority for work in your life?*
- *How does the proposal align with your current lifestyle, and plans for your lifestyle? Is it going to block any of your current aspirations?*

- *Will you be able to keep committed? What examples can you recall when you've been committed in the past? Are there any examples when your commitment has waned that you can learn from and avoid repeating?*
- *How does your openness to change and appetite for risk align with the proposal? Will you be able to make the decisions that are required?*
- *How strong is your attention to detail and organization? Will you be able to keep track of the admin and paperwork and stick to your plan?*
- *If the proposal requires access to sensitive information, is this something you're comfortable with?*
- *How complex is the work you'll be undertaking? Are you comfortable meeting customer expectations and doing what you say you're going to do?*

Understanding yourself is key to developing your thinking around your business investment. It's possible to weight some of these considerations and, as an example, a lack of experience may not necessarily be a blocker if you have the right skills and an appetite to learn.

The useful factor

The good news is you don't need to do everything yourself. In fact, if you tried, you'd likely end up exhausted and would deliver an inferior offering.

There are people out there to solve just about every problem you have when starting a business. Often they are freelancers available on a per-job basis with no long-term commitments who can save you time (and therefore money) or improve your offering by providing skills you don't have. This will allow you to focus your time on what you do best to add value to your business.

Consider a significant DIY job at home; if you're not a kitchen fitter by trade, you wouldn't dream of trying to fit a kitchen yourself – or, if you did, you'd accept it wouldn't look perfect and would take longer to complete than if installed by a professional.

Exactly the same principle applies to a social media campaign, for example. There are experts out there who know exactly how to engage with your target audience and to make an impact on what is a crowded space. Bringing the right people into your team and investing in them is likely to provide a return.

Action 0N

As part of your business case, identify what skill sets would be useful. Then, prioritize them as a high, medium or low requirement. Finally, capture an estimated cost and the forecasted benefit of using them. You can then decide whether the investment is justified.

Once you have identified a useful skill set that justifies investment to support your business, consider the following regarding individuals.

- *Do you know who they are?*
- *Do you know whether they want to work with you?*
- *Have you seen examples of the quality of their work, including validated reviews or recommendations?*
- *Do you know when they are available and does this align with your timeline?*
- *Is their cost in line with your estimate?*

From people that might never meet and can be spread across the world, it's possible for you to create a virtual team and harness a team ethic. You can introduce them to each other, hold virtual team meetings and set criteria for when you get involved to offer strategic input or approval of their work. This virtual team has the added benefits of being able to flex up or down to your business needs going forward and, depending on location and time zone, even to offer a global reach.

The timing factor

There is always a right time to make an investment, but that time may not be now, and it's not always obvious when the right time will be.

Markets can often change quickly, and what may have been a profitable gap one day may be filled by many others by the time you're ready to commit, therefore significantly reducing the attraction of the investment.

Looking at my own position, when we decided to make the leap to start a business with me as an independent consultant, it wasn't without risk (per the example in 'The impact factor', my wife Trang's support was a key part of the decision and I wouldn't have done it without her blessing). We were expecting our first child, and to some, including a former manager I later bumped into, the risk was seen as excessive and irresponsible.

But we had quantified it. The risk was low, and the window of opportunity was closing. As it was, our finances were in order and we were both earning a similar amount of money in permanent jobs. Either one of our salaries was enough to pay our monthly bills providing we were sensible with non-essential spending.

Therefore, ahead of Trang going on maternity leave, we understood it was low-risk and I had three to six months to secure a contract role, which I was confident I'd be able to achieve, especially being immediately available. If it hadn't worked the option would have existed to revert to a permanent role. In many ways, it was a free hit.

If we'd waited until the baby was born, with Trang on statutory maternity pay it would have been a much greater risk to branch into something new, and our savings would have quickly disappeared if I hadn't found a contract. With our circumstances changing, it might never have happened.

Windows of opportunity are often small, and if you're to maximize your opportunities it's vital you're clear on when they occur and what you need to do about it.

As it turned out, despite a few scary weeks running down my notice period and having no leads, and indeed the temptation of revoking my notice, as had been politely offered by my employer, I held my nerve and found a three-month contract starting on the Monday after leaving permanent work on the previous Friday. I'd put myself in a position to fail, raising all sorts of doubt and fear, but the timing was right, the risk was justified and we have never looked back.

Equally important on the timing side is to not put things on the 'never never' list. By this, I mean having a goal, but it being so remote you never get there, such as moving to another country in two years' time. Each year, it's easy to put this back a year. Then another year. Suddenly, you're five years down the line, and that move abroad is still two years away.

At times, I feared this book was on the 'never never' list. Even though I'd made some headspace to plan it, the challenge of combining it with client work and family life was ultimately too much.

Multi-tasking can be a challenge and even with the best intentions things began to slip, and I lost momentum. The project went in bursts of solid progress, followed by no progress, for about three years. I then made a clear commitment to myself that once the contract I was in had ended, the book would be my number-one focus – no exceptions, no distractions, and a clear deadline with my publisher.

Action 0O

Decide when the right time is to start. Consider the following.

- *When are you going to make the headspace so that you can do your best work and build the foundations that your business deserves?*
- *How do your current commitments align with your proposal?*
- *What future commitments or life events may impact your timing?*
- *What priority is this compared to everything else in your life?*
- *If applicable, when does the window of opportunity close due to personal circumstances?*
- *Is there a market-led case for quick or deferred action?*
- *When is your absolute deadline to start?*

The sales factor

The final step in the INPUTS Framework is your bread and butter – selling! You don't need me to tell you that without customers and making sales you won't have a business for long. You may think you have a valuable offering, but if not enough people want to buy it you'll be in serious trouble.

Action 0P

Conduct an analysis of the market that interests you, then consider where you fit in. This will give you clarity on the viability of your proposal. To do this, ask yourself the following.

The market

- *What market do you propose to go into?*
- *How much competition is there within the market?*
- *What are the supply and demand dynamics?*
- *How mature is the market?*
- *Is the market growing?*
- *How fast are trends moving in the market?*
- *Will your offering be in demand by the time you're ready?*
- *Is your market confined to a certain geography or can you sell worldwide?*

Where you fit in

- *What will your offering be?*
- *Will you sell the same offering throughout the year or account for seasonal trends?*
- *Who are you going to sell your offering to?*
- *How are you going to reach your customers?*
- *What is your unique selling point (USP)?*
- *Are you confident in selling yourself as well as your offering?*
- *Is there a social benefit you're passionate about that'll ensure you're the right person to sell it?*
- *Do you need to physically be there, or will you have an online shop?*
- *Does your offering scale or do your products and/or services need to be created individually, or even customized onto a base product?*
- *What future opportunities could this lead to or what doors could this open, including partnerships?*

Once you've gained clarity on the market and where you fit in, you should be in a position to complete the financial information required for the numbers factor.

Competition isn't always a negative. If someone has made a success of their business in a similar market this should give you the confidence you can too. Equally, in some markets, the same customers may use several suppliers, and your offering may end up being complementary rather than direct competition to others', which given time and the recognition of your presence in the market can lead to collaboration and partnerships. This is covered in more detail in Step 6: Expand.

Retrospective

From this pre-step, you should be clear on what visibility analysing the six INPUTS factors will give you and how this can provide clarity and confidence that you're making the right decision as you develop your business case during Phase 1.

Next, we'll consider whether investing time and energy into completing this analysis and developing a business case is right for you.

Signing off Phase 0

We've covered two very different frameworks in Phase 0. One is purely about you. The other is about your proposed business and what could change for you and the key people in your life.

Before moving on, you'll need to be comfortable that you've got your mindset SORTED and are clear on the INPUTS required to make a success of your project and business investment. This foundation will hold you in good stead moving forward.

The decision required is called a 'Go/No Go', which is as straightforward as it sounds. You either decide to go ahead and pass through the gate, or you decide not to.

Unlike the later phases of the project, when there are more stakeholders, only you can decide when you're in the position to go ahead and start planning your business. It may even be right now.

Once you decide that you're ready to start your project proper, if you haven't done so already, it's time to go public with your intention. That may simply be to discuss your ambition to start a business with your spouse, family or friends.

Making the right people aware (I appreciate it may not be the right time with some, such as an employer) will start to make it real and tangible and begin to make you accountable. The more accountable you are, the more likely it is to gain momentum and to happen. It's an exciting step, and one to be proud of.

Now, it begins. Let's start making the right decision!

Phase 1

Making the right decision

Initiating Phase 1

Phase 1 is about making the right decision. It consists of three distinct parts, the first three steps of the FUTURE Method. These are:

- Step 1: **F**ind something you may be interested in doing.
- Step 2: **U**nderstand why you think it could be the right fit.
- Step 3: **T**rial it to prove or disprove your thinking.

We'll go through them one by one, in detail, with actions and decisions flagged at the right time – as is the case throughout the FUTURE Method.

The three steps of Phase 1 are cyclical. It may be that, for example, finding a niche, understanding how it links to your values and trialling it by volunteering means the whole process has to be revisited. Or at least parts of it. There may be several cycles, some in parallel, depending on timelines and the decision to be made.

It's safe learning and exploring, without any big commitment, and it's better to know now than after you've fully committed to something that wouldn't have worked.

When you've completed the actions in Phase 1, you'll have made the decision on the future direction of your working life.

To help with that, let's look at making a project plan.

Making a project plan

Within your project, you'll make three plans – one each for Phases 1, 2 and 3. Before we look at the contents of your Phase 1 plan, let's look at planning more generally.

The value of having a strong plan cannot be overestimated. Your plan will show you where you're going and how you'll get there, and will give you visibility of whether you're on track or slipping behind. It will also give you clarity on your goals, your priorities, what tasks justify your attention and for how long.

It's easy to overlook the need for a plan, to spend a short period of time on it or to put it in the drawer and forget about it once it's been written. However, I strongly recommend you make your plan, keep it up to date and keep it in mind as part of your daily routine. The investment you put in developing it upfront, and keeping it accurate, will empower you to achieve your goals.

As you're developing your plan, there will be some trial and error. Focus on the goals you want to achieve and when you want to achieve them, and set key milestones to help achieve each goal.

A milestone is a point in time when you can check progress towards your goal. There may be a number of objectives to deliver ahead of the milestone. There should be a number of milestones, in sequence, that build up to delivering the goal within your project.

Once you have these milestones captured, working backwards from the goal will allow you to first see how realistic it is, and also to take it down a level and work out what objectives and smaller tasks are required to reach each of your key milestones. You can then flesh out your plan with this detail.

This approach should also enable you to capture your 'critical path', which consists of the tasks that cannot be delayed if you're to reach your target in an optimum way.

You'll have a capacity, and there is only so much that can be done, so plan your top-priority tasks first then work out the others around them.

It's highly likely that in this discovery period you'll identify some longer-term aspirations for Phase 2 or 3 of your project. They are absolutely worth capturing, first so they are not forgotten, and also to ensure they aren't prioritized too soon.

In terms of the level of detail within your plan, I've seen excellent short plans and dreadful long plans, and vice versa. You'll also only have so much information available as you start, especially for some of the longer-term activities, so try not to capture detail for the sake of it.

Size really doesn't matter; it's about the quality of the detail you include, how you work to stick to it and how you respond when things change.

Plans change – that's life, and that is fine, as long as you know when and how to respond. We cover more on that in Step 5: Review.

There are many different web-based tools out there to create a plan, but depending on the number of tasks you have it's also possible to use a spreadsheet.

Also worthy of note here is the daily 'to do' list. Making a simple list of things you plan to do each day will keep you focused and your mind clear. It's also incredibly satisfying to strike a firm line through them when they're done.

Plan

Each sub-step covered within the three steps of Phase 1 – Step 1: Find, Step 2: Understand and Step 3: Trial – is a potential category, or work-stream, to form the basis of your Phase 1 plan, and is food for thought as you build your business case. Some will be quick and easy for you to complete, whereas others will require deep thought and consideration.

These are the workstreams from which you'll build your project requirements. I explain requirements in more detail in Step 2: Understand.

It's worth noting that not all of these potential workstreams will be needed in your project. Some by default won't apply to you and the type of business you're looking to create, and that is absolutely fine. The key is to consider the question: 'does this apply to me?'. If the answer is 'no', mark it as not applicable, or n/a, and move on.

The biggest milestone in Phase 1, and of your entire project, is signing off your completed INPUTS business case document. Therefore, pick a deadline for that as soon as is appropriate. Also consider what other milestones will work for you in the interim to keep you accountable to yourself and on-track.

Confirming, or baselining, the plan once all tasks and milestones are understood will allow you to get on with delivering your objectives to meet your goals.

Step 1: Find

The scope

Whatever your background, it may feel as though your personal circumstances and the challenges you have to overcome are unique. However, I have learned that the journey to success as your own boss is a lot more predictable than you may think, and applying the principles defined here will lead to greater control and better decision-making.

There are more options available than ever before in how you can go about applying your skills and, indeed, learning new ones. This is an opportunity, but it can also be overwhelming. There are no wrong answers – apart from choosing something that isn't right for you.

In this step, you'll discover how to identify and develop candidate projects that may go on to form the basis for your business.

Before moving on, I introduce the concept of the Steering Committee, a decision-making forum. Then, we cover the agenda for an initial Steering Meeting where you'll decide which candidates to take forward to the next step.

Let's start finding!

The BIDS candidates

When kicking off a project, there is often little information to use, but there is a desired outcome. In my M&A career, a client would initially set a goal to grow or diversify their business, then begin looking for target businesses to acquire or merge with. In your case, it's about determining what meaningful problems you want to solve, why you have that goal, and finding navigable routes to achieve it.

There are many different answers and routes to get there. In this step, we focus on identifying them, then narrowing them down. This is done via a bidding process, as follows.

- Identify the high-level essence of a project.
- Create a candidate project.
- Compare it against alternatives.
- Decide what to take forward.

In my first project management role, in the banking sector, part of my weekly routine was to collate the project initiation documents, or PIDs for short. I had to ensure they had the right information included and then submit them for management review.

Each PID was not a fully scoped project; it was simply a one-page request – or bid – to spend time, effort and therefore money to research further. Many bids were submitted each week, and although the rate varied based on the quality of the bids submitted, perhaps only 20% were approved.

In your scenario, your ideas must bid for your attention, and you can formalize that here with your own BIDS candidate document.

The BIDS candidate can be a simple one-pager covering the following.

- **B**rief: what is it?
- **I**ntention: what are you looking to achieve, and why?
- **D**emand: who will you appeal to?
- **S**uccess: what examples are there of others who have succeeded here?

Creating many bids, you'll also see patterns emerge and ideas overlap. You can then rule out those that you decide not to take forward, or merge two or more into a feasible BIDS candidate.

You may choose to take forward more than one BIDS candidate during Phase 1, even ideas that are completely distinct. I recommend that you do, and I also suggest you remain open to the possibility of change and evolution throughout the journey.

Continuing to consider the 'do nothing' option of remaining where you are – even if you've decided you absolutely want to move on – will be useful as a tangible baseline with which to compare your ideas.

Action 1A

Create your simple BIDS candidate template and start capturing ideas. Keep this to hand and continue to iterate and refine as you progress through the actions of Step 1: Find.

The different options

In essence, there are three different options to life as your own boss: as an entrepreneur, freelancer or contractor. It may be that you're a combination of these, or that your company evolves over time, but let's look at them individually.

The entrepreneur starts a business that isn't necessarily about offering their specific skills. They develop assets. The business offers products and/or services that could be recognized as a distinct business with its own identity if the founder were to disappear. It may have many suppliers within the supply chain and may sell business-to-business (B2B) or business-to-consumer (B2C), or a combination of the two. An entrepreneur may require significant start-up finance or investment in order to get their offering to market. They may need facilities, branding and staff from the day they launch. Examples include a street-food van, a children's play café or a bespoke jewellery company.

The freelancer has a skill or trade that they may offer on a B2B or B2C basis. They tend to have few tangible assets beyond their own skill set. Often catering to many customers at a time, even on the same day, and often without the expectation of repeat business, the freelancer is someone who offers simple, repeatable, easy-to-understand services as a solution to the needs of their customers. Simple doesn't have to mean easy to replicate, however, and the niche nature of some free-lancers' services can result in a high price point.

It's normally quicker and simpler for someone to start as a freelancer than as an entrepreneur due to the nature of their offering. It may be that they can work remotely from anywhere in the world. They may not have a need for their own website and instead promote them-selves using marketplace websites like peopleperhour.com or fiverr.com. Examples include a photographer, illustrator, voice-over artist or almost any role within the 'gig economy'.

The contractor is similar to the freelancer, but most often operates at a B2B level only, with one client or a small number of clients at a time, and over a longer duration. Contracting offers the most similar working pattern to that of an employee, and often the contractor works within a team of employees filling a short-term skills gap or offering specialist skills the client may not require (or be willing to pay for) permanently due to a specific project or business need.

Contractors are paid a premium for their skills, their availability, their flexibility and their ability to parachute in and get things done. They often operate on a day rate rather than a price in exchange for deliv-ering specific tasks. Contracting work is, however, project-based and outcome-driven. This natural end point is what makes it different from the role of an employee.

If you're pondering contracting, consider the value you can add rather than the length of the contract. Even for a short project, you may offer significant value and be able to negotiate a high rate that is justifiable to your client due to the return they will receive on their investment in you.

The market for contractors varies by geography. In Singapore, for example, it's much smaller than in Britain. This is in part cultural but also due to the tax structure. Examples of a contractor include a project manager, IT developer or HR consultant.

Action 1B

It's likely you already know where you'll fit within this land-scape, but consider how this may evolve over time.

- *Do you envisage remaining as a freelancer or contractor for the long term, or is this a starting point before evolving into an asset-rich business like an entrepreneur?*
- *What would be the point at which you'd make the transition?*
- *If you're planning to be an entrepreneur, is there an opportunity to start sooner as either a freelancer or a contractor?*

Giving your project a name

Have you ever wondered why businesses give their projects a name?

A project name makes an idea tangible and real, and if it has an appropriate name computes the end goal into the minds of those responsible for delivering the project. This helps with focus and drive towards delivering that goal.

As you may have guessed, I called this book-writing project 'Project Future'. As I'd delayed the project for more than three years it almost felt like it was *always* going to be in the future, but the reasons for this name are many.

Yes, it's about a project and a method called 'FUTURE'. But more than that, it's about my future, as I pivot from being a contractor, offering my time for money where the main asset is my knowledge and experience, to having a more rounded business with tangible assets, such as this book and the courses I run that expand on many of the themes we touch on here. Most importantly, it's about your future, empowering you to deliver your own business project and achieve your goals, satisfaction and balance.

Action 1C

Think about what you're looking to achieve.

- *What is a key goal for you in one, two or three years' time?*

Play with project names accordingly. A good name is aspirational, and you'll be proud to share it with those who inevitably join you on your journey in one form or another.

Premature decision risk

You may think you know what business you want to create and that Step 1: Find doesn't apply to you. I advise strongly against that.

For a start, there is always a way of making it better! Assessing the idea is just as important as for someone who is less clear on their path – if not more so because other options may have been dismissed too easily.

It may be that your confidence is misplaced and you won't enjoy it as much as you think. The challenge could be too great, or too small. It could be too far removed from what you know, or not far enough.

Equally, you may have ruled an option out too soon as being beyond your level or not feasible that deserves more consideration.

Action 1D

Apply the INPUTS Framework to any strong ideas you have and keep it in mind as you consider the rest of this step. Keep your mind open to other opportunities, and capture them via the BIDS process to ensure the decision isn't a foregone conclusion.

Exploring all ideas

Whilst your ideas are simply that, it's easy to think again. Once you've committed time, money and energy to an idea, it's both harder and more frustrating to change course, so this is the time to invest in exploring all ideas.

Feel free to search out even the most abstract of things you're interested in, as I can almost guarantee somebody somewhere has monetized it and made a living from it.

Listening to podcasts and exploring YouTube, subject-specific news articles, blogs, Instagram profiles, Facebook groups, LinkedIn groups and online magazines can all be useful ways to expand your knowledge. This may result in a lightbulb moment where two seemingly unrelated streams converge, and an exciting opportunity arises that you hadn't considered previously. The deeper you dig, the more likely you are to find the right answer.

Consider your hobbies. What do you choose to do with your spare time? Is there a way you can combine this with some of your professional experience and monetize it? What work would you choose to do if qualifications, experience and pay were not relevant? Also, what would you do with your day if you didn't have to work?

If your idea is too big to start with, instead of abandoning it, consider how you can break it down into a more bite-sized chunk to get you started.

My wife, fine jewellery aficionado Trang Do, explains her experience.

> I had an idea to launch a jewellery marketplace, showcasing the products of many designers, to help people find a piece that's personal to them. It would've been a big task. To make it a success I would've needed upfront investment to help with financing, significant contributions from tech experts and also both suppliers and customers to engage.
>
> I did a lot of research and spoke with investors, who were open to the concept, but it didn't feel right. It was too much, too soon. So, I decided to break it down and start with something I know and love, which is fine jewellery, via my own brand, and use that as a step towards the marketplace. It has the same ethos of providing a personalized experience and heirloom-worthy jewellery that inspires.

Deciding which ideas to take forward, and the scale of them, isn't meant to be easy. It can be a real challenge, but equally it can be exciting and empowering. When considering ideas, nobody can hold you back apart from yourself.

Action 1E

Spend ten minutes writing freely about your aspirations for your business and your lifestyle. As you start, write at the top of the paper 'I would like my business to...', and see where your mind takes you before the time runs out. Once complete, you can get an insight of what is deep in your mind and explore why you're attracted to certain ideas. There may be some concepts and keywords to explore further that you hadn't considered previously.

Pivot

It's easy to think you've had enough of something and want to start afresh. Restarting, however, can be very painful. It takes you right back to the beginning and throws away the value you've built up.

If you're not careful, you can repeat the process of restarting and never truly succeed in any environment. What is much more valuable and strategic is to *pivot*.

To pivot is to use the skills and experience you've built up and apply them in a different way, or to a different market, whilst remaining aligned to your values and ambitions as you move forward.

By writing this book and setting up a business through which I empower people to launch a successful, independent career, I have pivoted from being a project manager in a corporate environment, delivering new products and services, to becoming a project manager in the self-help industry.

Everything I learned in that environment is applied in this: working with my clients to make a plan, mitigate risks and achieve their goals. I am still a project manager, but instead of having one client at a time I now have many clients and projects ongoing concurrently.

Similarly, when home cooking educator Dani Mosley decided she wanted a change after being a childminder for eight years, she considered retraining as a vet. But when discussing options with her husband, they spoke about her passion for food and sharing knowledge.

Dani was already doing this socially by sharing her family meal plans on Instagram. She considered working with parents at first, but she loved working with kids and had so many years' experience of doing so. Therefore, her business primarily educating children how to cook and understand food was born.

Action 1F

Think about your experience and what you know.

- *How can you pivot to apply this in what you want to do next?*

Be careful of the devil you know

As we covered in the sub-step 'Pivot' above, applying your experience to date, even loosely, will hold you in good stead and provide that kick-start. You'll already have credibility, the basis of a network, and it should mean there are people to support you on your way.

Having said that, you could play it too safe and simply end up repeating what you've done before and what, over time, has led to you becoming unfulfilled and wanting a change.

Looking at my own journey, right from the start I made safe choices based on the proverb 'better the devil you know than the devil you don't'. The problem was that I didn't know very much, and had such limited experience that being risk-averse in this way severely limited my options.

I'd chosen my degree based on what my best A-level grade was, rather than what I enjoyed doing. This ignored everything I was passionate about and the wider choice available, and it was not until the final year of university that I realized I would have been better studying international business or human geography, rather than the course I chose of business with law.

If I'd really thought it through, it would've been obvious that my child-hood interest in maps, people and places, and more recent interest in travelling, would have led to this conclusion when the decision was needed. I even had extra time to decide, having taken a year out before going to university.

I'd spent my year out working in admin at a law firm in London. I didn't have a particular interest in law, but I got a six-week summer job covering staff holidays, and I ended up being there for a year. Based on this, I chose to add the law element to my business degree, even though I still wasn't particularly interested in law. Looking back, it was crazy, but at the same time it directly linked to my biggest professional experience, and I knew no better.

A decade later, when I decided to become a contractor, it was time to be confident and stop playing it so safe. It would have been a lower risk for me to continue doing what I had the most experience in, and pitch myself as an IT project manager. I had spent most of my project management career in technology but had no real passion for it. Even when working within technology, I found I worked best with the business stakeholders, such as operations, as that's where my interest was.

Therefore, I was determined to use this opportunity to pivot and to get out of a technology environment. As so much of business is about relationships, I thought this would better allow me to enjoy my working life, but also to thrive.

So that was my initial thinking to pivot: remain as a project manager but steer clear of the technology devil I knew.

Action 1G

Think about your own decisions so far in your career.

- *Where have you played it too safe, and what have been the consequences?*
- *What could you have done differently that you can apply this time around?*

Finding a niche

A niche is a small segment of an industry within a wider sector. Niches exist for just about anything, so your challenge is to find one that you fit into and feel comfortable with. Your unique characteristics will make you stand out above others in this particular area, therefore making you desirable to potential customers.

It's your specialism and provides a starting point for developing your offering and unique selling point (USP). Taking this one step further, a micro-niche is a smaller segment within a niche.

Being a specialist or focusing on a niche doesn't need to restrict your options. It's possible to focus on various revenue streams or markets whilst being true to the niche that helped you appeal to customers in the first place.

Finding a niche is becoming ever more critical. Early in my career, I focused on being an all-rounder – competent with numbers and writing, flexible, working in big companies and small, having generic qualifications. In order to stand out and succeed in the new global economy, you'll need to shout, 'this is what I do; this is why you need me'.

It may be that your niche comes to you by accident. Before launching his own independent career, e-commerce specialist Martin Duffy had been working *ad hoc* as an audio technician supporting live music shows. He told me what happened next.

> *I enjoyed it, and found the pay was higher on a pro rata basis than my nine-to-five job, so I decided to get into it full-time. I knew it was never going to be perfect due to the travel and anti-social hours, but I decided to take the chance.*
>
> *Almost as soon as I did, the work dried up and I quickly realized I needed an alternative source of income. I understood the accessories used to support audio in stage shows, and the distributors of the products, so I decided to start selling parts online via eBay. Unexpectedly, this became an immediate success. My knowledge of the products enabled me to offer bespoke customer service, rather than simply repeating the 'out-of-the-box' instructions so many sellers offer.*

Martin decided to stop the audio technician work and focus 100% on selling via eBay, Amazon and his own website. His concerns regarding travel and anti-social hours were gone, and he was in business offering a great service within his niche.

Action 1H

Write down your ten favourite websites/sections of websites, companies and people you aspire to be like.

- *Is there a theme?*

Explore the internet to encircle ideas, and you may find an exciting niche that is right for you.

Not reinventing the wheel

It's easy to think that to be successful you have to find something new, but the niche you choose doesn't have to be empty. In a way, everything has been done now. If you're looking at a market that is completely empty, it may be that the market doesn't exist, or that the adoption period for your audience to accept it as necessary means the timing isn't right for you.

You don't need to reinvent the wheel to find your niche. If you're good at what you do, offer desirable products or services balanced at the right price, quality and convenience and make enough potential customers aware that you exist, you can succeed even in the most crowded market.

Equally, it may be that what you offer isn't anything new – you're just the one to put it out there for an audience that may not be well served.

Martin Duffy explains from his experience.

> *It can be very easy to talk yourself out of an idea. Don't obsess over finding a gap in the market. Give it a try and see how it goes. You'll soon realize what you can offer that others don't.*

Action 1I

Consider what common products or services appeal to you.

- *What angle do you have that can make you stand out?*
- *Is there a geography or audience that is not well served where you can claim that space as your own?*

Aiming higher

Before you get too far along your journey, recognize if you're setting the bar too low.

We've looked at the importance of enjoying work rather than enduring it, and how setting yourself goals will keep you motivated. It may be that the bids you put forward are too simple and easy to achieve.

That is fine as a starting point – you've got to start somewhere – but if that is the case, before proceeding check that there is a natural next step within the niche you're considering. If there is, plan for that and use the data in your initial bids to plan your early actions. If there isn't, consider if it's right for you to continue.

As with everything in life, you only get what you'll settle for. The better your business, the more satisfied you'll be.

Action 1J

Look at your initial BIDS candidates and see how you can add a minimum of 10% – be that in quality, margin or volume – or a combination of them.

- *Is it something you can scale?*
- *Are there other markets or complementary products or services you could add to your offering?*

The Steering Committee

As we get to the end of Step 1: Find, it's time to introduce the concept of a Steering Committee, or SteerCo.

In a corporate environment, a SteerCo is a group of senior stakeholders with responsibility for the different areas of the business impacted by a project. They meet regularly during the lifecycle of a project to receive a progress update and to ensure it is going in the right direction. They make decisions, and can also request a change of direction if things aren't going well.

This concept will also work for you, but less formally, in the shape of an advisory board. To give it the status it deserves within your business, though, we'll also call it a SteerCo.

When deciding who should be on your SteerCo, consider who is appropriate to support your decision-making. Looking at the impact factor, you may wish to include your spouse or a family member. If you're thinking of starting a business with a partner, it should absolutely include them. You might have a trusted friend or colleague who has been through this journey in the past that you'd like to include, or a mentor.

Numbers can vary, but I suggest your SteerCo be at least you and two others to ensure various angles are considered before making key decisions.

Once you've agreed on your SteerCo members, bring them up to speed on the nature of your project – what you're looking to achieve, the timeline and the responsibilities you'd like them to have. Are they an advisor or a decision-maker? Regardless of the decision-makers you have, there must be a chairperson to take ultimate responsibility, and that should always be a director – so you or your business partner.

Communicate clearly the dates for meetings and the agenda. You may send out pre-read materials, then after the meeting distribute outputs including decisions, next steps and the date of the next meeting.

If possible, I suggest you arrange a time and meet in person with all members of your SteerCo and talk through the agenda. You don't need to wear a business suit or book an office, but get the setting right, where you can focus on achieving the outputs you need. It may be a coffee shop or at home, but make sure it feels formal and structured. If it's not possible to meet in person then a group video conference call will ensure the right level of formality and debate.

Your SteerCo will be invaluable in discussing your plans, making decisions and capturing next-step actions and any risks.

Action 1K

Consider who should be on your SteerCo and their role and responsibilities within it. Ask them to join, and clarify your expectations of them. Decide your preferred venue and how you'll communicate dates, agendas and meeting outputs.

Steering Meeting 1: Signing off your BIDS candidates

Your very first Steering Meeting should be to sign off the BIDS candidates you're to take forward. Passing through this gate will result in an initial endorsement to commit further time, energy and potentially a small amount of funding to understanding those business ideas in more detail.

As part of your Phase 1 plan, capture a key milestone of when you expect to make your decision on which bids to take forward and schedule your Steering Meeting. The risk of analysis paralysis – where you effectively over-analyse a situation indefinitely with no decision ever taken – means there must be an endpoint to Step 1: Find, and committing to this deadline with those on your SteerCo will help you make it happen.

It's a key step, and one you should be proud of. To reach this stage you'll have developed the right mindset, made some headspace and completed some analysis of what you want to do with your future. From now on it's just about refining things and digging deeper.

Retrospective

From this step, you have discovered how to identify, develop and sign off candidate projects that may go on to form the basis for your business.

We've also covered the concept of a Steering Committee, and how you'd use that forum to make strategic decisions – starting with signing off your BIDS candidates.

Hopefully, you've expanded your thinking and opened up to some new ideas you hadn't considered, or improved on your original ideas.

Consider how applying the SORTED Framework has opened your mind to the wider possibilities that exist and what you could achieve.

Let's now move on to look at understanding *why* your candidates may or may not be right for you.

Step 2: Understand

The scope

At this stage, you'll have at least one candidate, and you're looking to learn more about it and develop your business case.

This step is key to driving the structure of your proposed business and proving the concept to yourself before you introduce it to any customers. It requires deep analysis from you and brutal honesty about the viability of your candidates, and how they'll develop into a business case proposal. For that reason, we'll refer to your candidates as your proposal from now on.

As there is so much here, it's broken down into three chunks.

Initially, we look at the *business environment* you'll enter. We consider the tools, processes and strategic options you can use to understand and develop your proposed business.

Next, starting with 'Finding the sweet spot', we look at *your own motivations* as to why you're proposing this business, and understanding how you can make the business work for you.

Then, starting with 'Training options', we look to understand what you can *learn from others* who have already made an impact in this market – both for you to learn from and collaborate with.

I make no apology that this step is designed to challenge you. It's this deep understanding that will go a long way to building a strong business that's right for you.

At the end of this step there is your second Steering Meeting. If that goes well and you're happy, you can move on to trialling your proposed business in the real world. If it doesn't, it's back to the drawing board and Step 1: Find.

Be in no doubt, though – both outcomes constitute success. If you validate your proposal enough to move on, that should give you confidence moving into Step 3: Trial. If, on the other hand, you decide not to progress with your current proposal (or proposals), then you've avoided a big mistake by not starting the wrong business.

Let's start understanding!

Requirements and design

After a project is given initial approval – in your case, signing off your BIDS candidates at Steering Meeting 1 – the next step is to broaden it out into something more tangible. This is done by developing requirements and designing how it will happen. This is essentially the *what* and the *how*, and should be governed by the *why*.

The requirements you choose will be the necessary elements to create a balanced and healthy business and lifestyle. As we covered in 'Making a project plan' above, each requirement should be tied to a category, or workstream, for which you can use the sub-steps in this book as a starting point.

The value in developing and clarifying your requirements is that this will define what is included in your plan, and, just as importantly, what isn't. Looking at this strategically will allow you to determine the scope of your proposed business, and whether it will work for you.

Here, you're the key stakeholder and ultimately will determine what is in scope and what isn't, but look to work with some others in this exercise, possibly members of your SteerCo. You may develop the requirements yourself initially or complete the whole exercise in a group.

There are lots of ways of developing requirements, but the method I've always found most useful is via a requirements workshop. In a corporate environment, a group of people with the right skills and knowledge for the project would sit down in a structured meeting.

They would take the end goal and work out what is required to get there, breaking down the requirements individually then grouping, sizing and prioritizing them. Let's look at these separately.

- *To group.* You may find similar requirements emerge, or ones that naturally follow on from each other. There may also be duplication, or more than one way of getting to the same goal, which you can work through and choose the right option. They may be in the same workstream or in various work-streams, with a dependency on one task being completed before another can start.

- *To size.* Requirements in software development are often simply sized as the amount of effort needed to complete them, but this may be broader for you. It could also cover the type of skills required that you need to source externally or the lead time if you have a dependency on suppliers, shipping time etc. Consider this as you build your plan. Partly based on this complexity, estimate the size of each requirement, like a t-shirt, into large, medium or small categories.
- *To prioritize.* Once you know the size of your requirements, the priority of each requirement will allow you to build your plan and understand your critical path. Split your requirements into three buckets for Phase 1, 2 or 3, just like your wider project. Initially, for requirements in Phase 1, prioritize them as high, medium or low. You'll then have clarity on where your attention should be.

A big pen and a bunch of Post-it notes are often all that is required to capture the initial requirements, and they can be developed in more detail away from the workshop.

Your requirements should be broken down into three different types. These are as follows.

- *Strategic requirements.* They are the goals and objectives that your business will plan to achieve, and how you'll achieve them. Example: 'The business MUST sell to customers in the UK and USA'.
- *Visible requirements.* They are how your business will look and feel. Example: 'The business MUST have its own website and brand identity'.
- *Personal requirements.* They cover how the business should facilitate your lifestyle and those included in your impact factor. Example: 'The business MUST NOT operate during the month of August'.

It's possible to have hundreds or even thousands of requirements. I once worked on a project that had over 8,000! To avoid over-complicating things, keep these to the minimum amount necessary.

In a technology environment, design often comes after the requirements are set, but for your business, you may be able to manage the two hand in hand. You'll certainly be able to work out the design of some yourself, whereas others, such as a website or marketing campaign, may need external support. This can be assessed on individual merits, and if you think the design fundamentally changes the requirement or the size of it, you can revisit the requirements process until satisfied.

Initially, your requirements will likely develop as you learn more about your project and proposed business. Work out how long you need to get clarity on your key requirements for Phase 2 (Step 4: Undertake and Step 5: Review) and ensure this is aligned to your business case when you're ready to review it for sign-off. This will ensure you retain focus on the right things during Phase 2 and don't get side-tracked by new things that'll inevitably come along – commonly known as 'scope creep'.

Action 2A

Plan your requirements workshop and start gathering what your business needs, what your customers need in order to engage with your business and what you need from your business. Decide the workstreams you'll focus on and any that are not required for your business, or are not a near-term priority.

Exciting times

Now is such an exciting time in history to become your own boss. The structure of the economy has changed beyond all recognition since the turn of the millennium. Wholesale improvements in technology, and the disruption it causes, have offered huge opportunities for nimble newcomers to take market share from established businesses by doing things better. This lack of stability is *your* opportunity.

The cost of starting a business and entering a marketplace, and the irrelevance of geography in many situations, has changed how the world works. It has never been easier to start a business and put your flag in the ground.

Barriers to entry in many industries have been removed or at least reduced. You can now base yourself anywhere and operate a small business, globally, with little more than a laptop and an internet connection.

A threat to consider is that others can do the same anywhere in the world. They have the same access to technology, and possibly a lower cost base.

Equally, if you decide you want to build a business locally, you can harness this technology to nurture and interact with your community.

Digital transformation will continue to accelerate in the years ahead, and even the most traditional of businesses would benefit from some online presence to interact with customers and provide a base of information to become known, liked and trusted. It's your platform.

Action 2B

When reviewing your initial proposal, consider the following.

- *What is a growing trend and what is being replaced?*
- *What opportunities are there now?*
- *What is likely to grow in the years to come?*
- *What gap in the market do you see?*
- *How can you avoid being undercut on price by a competitor in a lower-income economy? Will you offer quality or convenience to remain competitive?*
- *How can you be a disrupter and take market share from competitors who have more resources and a bigger reputation?*

SWOT analysis

The SWOT analysis is a simple tool with four boxes covering strengths, weaknesses, opportunities and threats. Its enduring popularity is due to its simplicity in capturing the emphasis of what can help or hinder a business, both internally within the company and considering the external environment.

Let's look at each box in turn.

- *Strengths* are what you think your business should be known for and where you can stand out. They are internal attributes and are helpful for you to achieve your objectives and goals. Identifying strengths gives you the insight to focus on building them further and positioning your business on them.

- *Weaknesses* are areas of concern where your business would benefit from being stronger. Like strengths, they are internal attributes, but they are harmful as you aim to achieve your objectives and goals. Identifying weaknesses will allow you to understand them and focus on areas of improvement, or position your business away from them.

Both strengths and weaknesses can come from a number of sources, including your own skill set, knowledge, experience or network, or any characteristics about the products or services you plan to offer.

- *Opportunities* offer a chance to grow your business. They are external attributes, linked to the market and wider society, and are helpful for you to achieve your objectives and goals. Being aware of opportunities and taking the right ones is likely to be critical to the success of your business.
- *Threats* are a challenge to your business. Like opportunities, they are external attributes, linked to the market and wider society, but they are harmful as you aim to achieve your objectives and goals. How you overcome threats will be critical to the success of your business.

Both opportunities and threats have the ability to take you by surprise. They can appear quickly, and whilst the opportunity can also disappear quickly, the threat could make a big impact in a short time if the risk is not mitigated. They could come from your competition, government regulation, a change in consumer habits or many other sources.

Action 2C

Draw your own SWOT diagram and start to plot what you see as key factors for the bids you've taken forward to form your proposal.

- *What has this taught you about the strategic priorities of your proposed business?*
- *What objectives and goals can you set as a result?*
- *Has it reinforced your thinking or are you having to change tack?*

Managing risk

As a project manager, there are two documents I rely on daily. The first is the plan; the second is the risk log.

The risk log normally forms part of a wider document, called a RAID log, that also includes assumptions, issues, and dependencies.

The RAID log is used as a control tool. In a corporate environment, the project manager uses it to gain confidence from stakeholders that they are indeed in control.

The RAID log should be used for the duration of your project, normally at each review; however, it's useful during Step 2: Understand to support the findings of your SWOT analysis and complete a scan of your wider environment. It will enable you to quickly identify and act upon any challenges that occur.

A summary of each is as follows.

- **R**isks are problems that haven't occurred yet but would have a negative effect if they did. Once they occur, a risk becomes an issue. Your task is to *mitigate* them. Example: 'There is a risk that supplier costs will be higher than planned'. Mitigation: break down costs per project line and review supplier agreements.

- **A**ssumptions are unknowns, where you assume a certain result to take place once they occur. Assumptions are effectively gaps in knowledge and are therefore a risk to your control of the project. If your assumption is incorrect, a risk arises. Your task is to *challenge* them. Example: 'The supplier will want to work with me'. Challenge: work closely with the decision-maker at the supplier to find out if your assumption is correct. Be upfront about volumes and costs, and make it formal.
- **I**ssues are risks that have occurred. They are currently causing a problem and need resolution if they are not to delay or negatively impact your project. Your task is to *resolve* them. Example: 'There is an issue that supplier costs are higher than planned'. Resolution: work with the supplier to renegotiate, find an alternative supplier, consider revising product quality, price, margin or availability.
- **D**ependencies are an external reliance on others to deliver in order to meet your requirements. Your task is to *manage* them. Example: There is a dependency on the supplier to ship the prototype six weeks before an event to ensure it's available to present to potential customers. Management: work closely with the supplier to ensure everything is on track to avoid a nasty surprise.

Like requirements, it helps to size risks. This will allow you to prioritize what is absolutely critical and what can wait. The simplest way is to consider both the impact if the risk occurred, and the likelihood of the risk occurring.

They are often categorized into high-, medium- and low-risk and displayed as the traffic light colours of red, amber and green, known as a RAG status. Also consider the proximity of the risk occurring, with priority on those that could occur in the short term. This also works for the other parts of the RAID log, although an issue log only has impact, not probability or proximity, as the issue has already occurred.

There are various ways of closing down a risk. Some are simply facts that you can't change. These are considered 'accepted' and are worth keeping your eye on. Once others are resolved, I tend to mark them as 'complete' and filter off the log, so the focus is on what matters going forward. I never delete – you never know when a similar problem will happen again.

Action 2D

Put together a RAID log and capture your current risks, assumptions, issues and dependencies, sizing and prioritizing their RAG status and their impact, probability and proximity as appropriate.

- *How has this changed your thinking about your proposed business and your priorities?*

Understanding your core customer

People primarily buy things for one very simple reason – they have a problem they want resolved. The problem is displayed in the form of 'something they need' or 'something they want'.

Your target audience, or core customer, is the person or type of business that your offering will most appeal to, and they'll look to you to resolve their problem. Your task here is to identify them. There will be more than one of them, but consider that you're serving an individual rather than a community.

If you target everyone, then chances are you'll appeal to nobody. Understanding who your core customer is will give you direction and clarity on your approach.

We've said that your niche is *what* your business does, but this should be considered alongside *who* it appeals to and, most importantly of all, *why* it appeals to them.

Understanding your core customer will allow you to develop products and services that solve a meaningful problem they have. It will also provide a platform for branding and communications to ultimately get their attention.

The better you understand your core customer, the deeper the relationships you're likely to build with them and the more successful you're likely to be.

When you're choosing your core customer, ensure you're appealing to the customer that is right for you, aligned to your own values. Having this chemistry and empathy will make your communication and sales natural and authentic. You want them to believe the same things that you do. You want to find the problem as meaningful as they do, and you should feel satisfaction when you've solved it for them.

Every type of customer exists, and compromising your values to serve a bigger market may be a false economy. A mismatch here could negatively impact your motivation to sell and their motivation to buy. It's a balance, though, as the market needs to be big enough for your business to make the impact you want.

Action 2E

Get a deep understanding of your core customer. Give them a persona. Draw a picture of them, name them, give them an age, gender, family status, job title and income. Consider the following.

- *Who are they?*
- *Where do they live?*
- *What are their needs?*
- *What do they aspire to?*
- *What motivates them?*
- *What problems or concerns do they have that you want to solve?*
- *What keeps them awake at night?*
- *What personality traits make them stand out and appeal to you?*
- *Who influences them?*
- *What do they do with their spare time?*
- *What media do they read, watch and listen to?*
- *What social media channels are they on?*
- *How do they make decisions?*
- *How can you solve their problem?*
- *Is there enough demand to justify the investment in them?*

Business complexity

What could be considered a risk is the complexity of your proposed business. Some businesses are straightforward, whereas others can be extraordinarily complex.

The simpler your business is, the more likely your customers are to understand it, the value you offer and why they should buy from you. This will deliver focus and get your message across. It will become what you're known for.

When my family and I spend time in Vietnam, my mother-in-law often takes us to the best restaurants. But these aren't what you might think. There is nothing five-star about them. They are often simple operations that just sell one dish. You sit down, and within a minute a delicious meal is served. Often the only variable is how much chilli or garlic you add – but that's on the table so no need for questions or staff involvement. The only option is the choice of drinks.

The reason this works is that the small business, with limited resources, focuses its energy on making one dish spectacular. If it's Phở noodle soup, for example, the broth could have been cooking for 12 hours and have received expert attention throughout. Customers will know such a place for the best Phở in the district, and will keep coming back as a result.

Action 2F

Consider how you can simplify your supply chain as much as possible between you and your customers. Consider the structure of your proposed business.

- *How many products and services do you plan to offer?*
- *What is the core product or service that you want to be known for?*
- *How many markets do you plan to serve?*
- *Are you planning to work business-to-business (B2B), business-to-consumer (B2C) or a combination of the two?*

If you're offering products or services, or both, consider these variables.

- *Will you sell as a one-off or have repeat customers?*

- *How big is the investment they need to make in you?*
- *How easy is it for your customers to say yes?*
- *How can you make it clear they should come to you to resolve their problem?*
- *Will you have a consistent business with revenue throughout the year, or a seasonal one, with a different offering, or even significant downtime, throughout the year?*
- *Is the success of your business weather-dependent, and if so, how can you mitigate this?*
- *If one product or market takes a downturn, how strong will you be in other areas to ensure your business isn't overly compromised?*

In addition, specifically if you're offering products, consider the following.

- *Will you have many or few suppliers in your supply chain?*
- *What options do you have for alternatives if a supplier fails you?*
- *How complex is the production process and what control do you have over it?*

And if you're offering services only.

- *Do you own all aspects of the services or are you working with others?*
- *If you're working with subcontractors, how can you be confident they'll continue to offer what you need them to?*

Competitive differentiators

When planning your business, you'll need to decide how and why you differentiate yourself from your competition.

There are three differentiators to choose from: quality, convenience and price. Successful companies almost always focus on one differentiator and never sacrifice on this. It's possible to have a minor focus on a second differentiator, but this should very much be secondary in your planning beyond your primary focus.

It's impossible to focus on all three; if you choose to do so, you'll offer too much for too little, not make enough profit and ultimately fail.

Getting clear on your approach to this will enable you to plan strategically regarding your offering, your pricing and how you'll present yourself to your customers.

Let's consider them one by one.

- *If you choose to compete on quality* by having the best products or services available with the greatest number of features, your customers will accept paying more and/or waiting for it. Example: you can spend years waiting for some Rolex watch models to become available, and this isn't due to any delay at the factory. The quality is high, but so is the price, and it's certainly not convenient to wait several years for a product. Yet due to the quality, the demand exists. The scarcity is deliberate and helps keep the price high.
- *If you choose to compete on convenience* your customers will accept a lack of quality or a higher price point. Example: I once had a contract based in the former media village at the Olympic Park in London. It was a shuttle-bus ride to the huge Westfield shopping centre, with lots of high-quality or cheap lunch options. Just outside the office door, however, there was a street-food pizza van. I wouldn't say it was the best quality, but it wasn't too bad. The price was more expensive than the pizza chain restaurant in the shopping centre, but my co-workers and I kept going back because it was incredibly convenient. The convenience of not getting on that bus outweighed the lower quality and higher price of the product.
- *If you choose to compete on price* by being the cheapest, your customers will accept lower quality and that it won't always be available. I'm sure you don't need me to share an example of a company that competes on price. This approach also comes with a health warning: competing on price often results in poor brand loyalty and also forces you to consistently focus on keeping the costs in your supply chain down. As a new entrant, it can be especially difficult to compete with established competitors due to the economies of scale they can achieve in their supply chain. I'm not saying don't choose this option, but I suggest thinking seriously about the type of business you want to build and if there's a better alternative.

Action 2G

Look at your proposal(s) and consider focusing on each differentiator in turn, with a 'minor' of one of the other two. For example – major on quality, minor on convenience, accepting price will be high (but justified). Think about how you can develop this into a wider strategy. For examples and inspiration, when watching television or listening to the radio, evaluate the messages of the adverts and how those businesses are communicating their differentiation strategy to potential customers.

Finding the sweet spot

In the Introduction, we looked at the catalyst that has made you consider becoming your own boss. Every new business owner will have slightly different motivations for their decision. Here, we dig deeper into why you're looking at the options currently in front of you and, in doing so, we find the sweet spot.

As you develop your proposal by understanding your BIDS candidates in detail, ask yourself the following questions.[1]

- What do I *love doing*?
- What am I *good at*?
- What does the *world need*?
- What can I be *paid for*?

At the intersection of these four questions, there will be a sweet spot where they converge – and there could be your answer.

Use your current (or most recent) job as a baseline study. Does it allow you to utilize your core strengths? Do you get satisfaction from solving the problems you care about? Once you have your baseline,

---

[1] Adapted from the Zuzunaga Venn Diagram of Purpose; see Zuzunaga, Andres (2011). 'Proposito'. www.cosmograma.com/proposito.php.

consider each of the BIDS candidates you've taken forward in turn and capture the relevant outputs in your draft business case proposal.

Be aware, however, that not all boxes are the same size, and not all circumstances allow for the perfect balance. There is a need to be pragmatic, and perhaps patient.

That is where weighting comes in. In order to make sense of this, I suggest creating a simple calculation: percentages always add up to 100%, and here you have four considerations. Start with 25% for each, then weight them according to your priorities – although all four remain needed to some degree for it to work.

For example, if you have a family to support and a big mortgage, you may need to compromise on doing something you love and focus on what you can be paid for. In this scenario, though, look to weight what you love doing as much as you can whilst being pragmatic – it will make your business better, keep you motivated and work towards your passion in your longer-term plan:

- what you love doing = 20%
- what you are good at = 30%
- what the world needs = 10%
- what you can be paid for = 40%

In another scenario, if your outgoings are low and you aren't neces-sarily looking to make a huge amount of money, focusing on what you love doing and what the world needs are likely to be more relevant to you than what you can get paid substantially for, so you may choose to weight it as follows:

- what you love doing = 35%
- what you are good at = 25%
- what the world needs = 30%
- what you can be paid for = 10%

The world is never static, and neither should your weighting be. I was pragmatic when I started my first business as a contractor – I had to be, with a baby on the way – but at the same time I saw it as an opportunity to get out of a technology environment, which I achieved successfully within a year or so as I transitioned to working in M&A, and then on to what I've decided I absolutely love doing, which is working with people like you to make a serious plan and achieve your own business goals.

To many on the outside, my decision to become a contractor appeared to be driven by money. Although a perk, this wasn't my main motivation. In the short term, what was much more important to me was the variety of my work. I had always moved around in my early career. Every move was strategic and well thought-through, but the thought of staying somewhere for too long was never a positive for me.

When I became senior enough to move onto a three-month notice period I didn't feel relief at the security; rather, I felt uncomfortable and trapped. I felt my hands were tied and I was inflexible, that if other opportunities were to come along I wouldn't be in a position to take them.

As we've seen when looking at 'The different options' in Step 1: Find, contractors are paid a premium, in part due to their flexibility and lack of job security – the convenience for the client – so as this type of work was my preference, it was an easy decision when the time was right.

And for the long term, it was also the foundation to learn about running a business before personalizing it into one in my sweet spot.

Action 2H

- *Out of the four areas that make up the sweet spot, what weighting would you give each at the moment?*
- *How does this change your thinking about your proposal?*

Lifestyle

It's an assumption not mentioned until now that you'll be looking to create a business to suit your lifestyle (or the lifestyle you want to have) rather than the next unicorn business.

In the 'Exciting times' sub-step above, we looked at how it's now possible to operate a small business, globally, due to modern technology. The same technology also means your working pattern doesn't need to be a rigid Monday-to-Friday nine-to-five.

Unless you're a contractor with a specified client, when it can be more like a regular job, your working pattern can be whatever you want it to be, as long as these boundaries are understood by your customers in advance.

You're in charge here, and you can set your business up in a way that works for you.

When home cooking educator Dani Mosley started her business, a primary focus was on creating a lifestyle that worked for her and her family. Dani, whose husband also runs his own business, explains.

> *It's about quality of life for us, and that's precisely why we do what we do. We can dip in and out, we can be there for our children, we can finish early if we need to. We have that flexibility and I plan the business around the children's needs.*

I was similar to Dani. A key driver for me when I decided to pivot from my contract work was the desire to be largely geographically neutral, without the need to stay away from home regularly. Yes, I host and attend physical events, but it's now the exception rather than the norm. I can plan business around my lifestyle choices and family commitments most of the time.

Looking from a slightly different angle, the architects who drew up the plans for our extension were a partnership of two, and they clearly defined, in large red text on the footer of every email they sent, the long holidays they had planned throughout the year, which basically coincided with school holidays.

They also explained before engaging their services that if the project was not completed before one of these holidays there would be nobody in the office and it would have to wait. This approach was direct, even abrupt, but it was also clearly communicated and as the client I could either agree (which I did) or look elsewhere. They understood it was feasible to run their business in that way, providing there were no surprises for their clients.

> ## Action 21
>
> - *What size of business do you want to achieve?*
> - *What flexibility do you want for your lifestyle?*
> - *How do you want your working day, week, month and year to be structured?*
> - *Can your proposal facilitate the lifestyle you're looking to achieve?*

Values

Now is your chance to build a business that places your values at the forefront of everything it does. Sounds exciting, doesn't it?

In a corporate environment, we often hear managers talk about company values, plastering them over the walls. One place where I worked even had them up and down the stairwells. Values are often met with cynicism, but only if they are a veneer rather than the true face of a company. What they say their values are and the reality can often vary significantly.

Values come first, then the culture of the company comes from the values that are lived day by day. If you get your values right, you'll most likely build a business where you're personally satisfied with the contribution you make in the world. In time you'll also attract like-minded people who want to be part of that journey with you.

It isn't necessarily easy to define what your values are, but looking into your past and realizing when you were happiest, what achievements you're most proud of and when you've felt most fulfilled is a good place to start. Use both personal and work examples.

My top three values at present are:

- *family* – because everything I do is for my family
- *accomplishment* – because I enjoy making things happen and seeing people succeed
- *honesty* – because nothing sustainable is ever achieved through dishonesty

It's normal that values can change over time, and often this takes place as you move into a new phase of your life. Your values right now might not be the same as they were five years ago, or indeed what they'll be in five years' time. Recognizing this change will enable you to align your working life with your values.

Agri-food innovator Ryan Edwards is an old friend of mine. We met during our university work placement year in 2004 and I've followed his career closely since. When climbing the corporate ladder, success (characterized by money and status) was a key value for him. Ryan was successful and reached a position in which he was comfortable financially. He bought a BMW, the car he'd always aspired to. Then, after having it for three days, he told me he was bored with it.

His values had changed, and it was this action that made him see it. Ryan explains.

> I realized it's just a car, and overnight my whole outlook on linking work to money changed. I realized I wanted enough money to not worry about it, but after that's achieved, I see no benefit in getting more. What would an upgrade on the BMW be, a Porsche? What value is there in me working for that?

And so, Ryan decided to change his career and accept an offer to manage a start-up in a field he had a passion for. Once he felt confident enough in the start-up world, he set up his own company based on his values of fun, empowerment and fresh thinking.

Action 2J

- *What are the top three values that define you, and how can you build those into the fabric of your business?*
- *How can you ensure the business stays true to those values or updates them as you grow?*

Purpose, mission and vision statements

Perhaps the biggest question of all is *why?*

The definition is often blurred, but there is a distinction between a purpose, a mission and a vision of a business. Getting clarity on these and being specific, clear and concise will help you understand why you're considering your proposed business, what it will do and where you'll aim to be.

The three statements can be summarized as follows.

- A *purpose* statement expresses the reasons the business exists.
- A *mission* statement expresses what the business does, and for whom.
- A *vision* statement expresses the desired future state of the business.

Before setting up her business, home cooking educator Dani Mosley saw a problem. Dani explains.

> *At the moment we're seeing trends of people just putting a ready meal in the microwave or getting a takeaway. This has so many negative results, including increased levels of childhood obesity. I also passionately believe that the meal at the end of each day, sitting around a table with your family, is such an important part of your day, coming together. So many families eat separately now in front of the TV or in shifts, or give different food to the children. I believe we need to get that family mealtime back as a priority. The meal plans I share on Instagram have been the foundation for me to write a family cookbook that will inspire more people.*

Breaking down everything Dani says above, we can see the following purpose, mission and vision.

- Dani's *purpose* is to reduce the prevalence of people eating unhealthily and eating alone.
- Dani's *mission* is to teach the next generation to learn to cook properly for themselves, to be inspired, to enjoy healthy food, to be open to a variety of flavours and to value spending time eating together as a family.
- Dani's *vision* is to grow her audience, increase her profile and write a family cookbook to share her message.

Leadership and life coach Sue Belton spoke to me about the value of recognizing your purpose, and how you'd identify it. Sue explains.

Purpose is for your life, not just your business. When you have your purpose and your values, they become your compass points by which you make decisions. Try to visualize it. Imagine that you've got one of those big billboards, and you can put whatever you want on that board. What would you put on it?

Action 2K

Create your own purpose, mission and vision statements. Understand why you're looking to create this specific business.

- *How does it link to your values?*
- *What is the problem you're looking to solve?*
- *How will you do it, and for whom?*
- *Once you're established, what is your vision for its growth?*

Visualize what you'd put on your billboard.

Personality types

Completing the self-evaluation exercise within the SORTED Framework will allow you to understand where you are in your career.

Recognizing your personality type will allow you to understand why you've succeeded in some areas and not in others.

There are many tools available to determine varied aspects of your personality. They are normally in the form of multiple-choice questions, with a personalized report being the output. Prices vary, and some are free. Here are some examples, with a summary of what they say about themselves.

- Myers-Briggs Type Indicator (MBTI).[2]

  The essence of the theory is that much seemingly random variation in behaviour is orderly and consistent, being due

---

[2] The Myers & Briggs Foundation (2020). 'MBTI Basics'. www.myersbriggs.org/my-mbti-personality-type/mbti-basics.

to basic differences in the ways individuals prefer to use their perception and judgement.

Possibly the most well-known personality test, the MBTI is based on the work of Carl Jung. There are 16 distinctive personality types based on a combination of four functions and four categories.

- Insights Discovery.[3]

Insights Discovery is built to help people understand themselves, understand others and make the most of the relationships that affect them in the workplace.

Like the MBTI, it's based on the work of Carl Jung and provides a detailed report of strengths using a four-colour model. My report places me in 'Fiery Red', meaning I am competitive, demanding, strong-willed, determined and purposeful.

- Belbin Team Roles.[4]

By using Belbin, individuals have a greater self-understanding of their strengths, which leads to more effective communication... Great teams can be put together... and everyone can feel that they are making a difference in the workplace.

This applies to you as your own boss, because you'll be required to put your team together, in whatever guise that takes – a key theme throughout this book. I undertook this test during my university work placement year, and my appointment into the 'Shaper' role was a defining aspect of my early career. It taught me both what I was and what I wasn't. I used this to make decisions moving forward. Project management is a natural 'Shaper' profession.

---

[3] Insights (2020). 'Insights Discovery'. www.insights.com/products/insights-discovery.
[4] Belbin (2020). 'What's Belbin All About?'. www.belbin.com.

- The Big Five personality test by 123test.[5]

  The Big Five personality test gives you more insight into how you react in different situations, which can help you choose an occupation.

  This free personality test measures your openness, conscientiousness, extraversion, agreeableness and neuroticism.

- Your Introvert Type: What Type of Introvert Are You?[6]

  This is a more specific test, and freely available. Authority on introversion Joanna Rawbone told me why she created this test.

  To help introverts better understand themselves, be confident with their introversion and step up authentically.

  As an only child, I've always felt comfortable spending time alone and I'd always partially considered myself an introvert, but at the same time I tend to be quite confident in a social setting. Taking this test made me understand more about myself, how I choose to engage and disengage. I am an introvert – a sociable, open, connected introvert to be precise – yet I have some connection preferences in common with many extroverts.

We are so close to ourselves; I've found these tools useful and each has taught me something different about myself. It's an opportunity to take a step back and evaluate your strengths and weaknesses. Looking deeper, you can consider what roles you should focus on delivering yourself, where you may need to improve and also where you should seek to outsource.

---

[5] 123test (2020). 'Big Five Personality Test Traits'. www.123test.com/big-five-personality-theory.
[6] Flourishing Introverts (2020). 'What Type of Introvert Are You?'. https://yourintroverttype.co.uk/.

Action 2L

Complete at least one personality test.

- *How do the results compare to what you expected?*
- *What can you learn from this to focus your business on your strengths?*
- *What can you consider stopping or outsourcing?*

Adaptive skills

Adaptive skills are skills that help a person adapt to a situation and make a success of it.

Behavioural skills specialist Chris Watson is the author of *Upskill: 21 Keys to Professional Growth*. In his book, Chris highlights the range of adaptive skills that, time and time again in a wide range of scenarios, result in positive professional growth.

I spoke with Chris about this and asked him which of these skills were most common amongst entrepreneurs, freelancers and contractors. Chris had completed a project for a client on this subject, and whilst the results reinforced the importance of all 21 adaptive skills, nine of them were consistently associated with individuals who demonstrated a more 'entrepreneurial mindset'. These were:

- ability to influence
- commercial thinking
- commitment to change and adaptation
- constructive communication
- creativity and innovation
- motivation to succeed
- positive decisions
- resilience and emotional control
- results through action

Chris told me that 'resilience and emotional control' particularly stood out, in almost every scenario.

In addition to these nine skills, a further two were regarded as relevant in certain scenarios. Of these more discretionary skills, it tended to be one or the other of:

- specialist knowledge and ability
- intuitive thought

Chris explains the relevance of these 11 skills for a new business owner.

For the first 12–18 months after starting a business, it's easy to get despondent. You haven't created much momentum yet, and as a result you're running at everything that could create a lead. If this happens, retaining a clear vision, commitment and demonstrating resilience and belief it will work – although not blind belief – are key to getting through the tough times.

Understanding the need for these skills doesn't mean you'll fail if you don't have them. Rather, if there are any gaps, are you aware of this? If so, how can you address them?

There are lots of ways you can address a skills gap – training, working with a partner or outsourcing the work to others are just three examples we'll cover later in this step.

Action 2M

Consider each of these 11 skills one by one.

- *Which of them do you consider to be particular strengths and weaknesses for yourself?*
- *How important are they to your business?*

Consider what action you'll take to resolve a skills gap.

Building or maintaining

The day-to-day activities you complete within your business can vary significantly, sometimes by making only minor tweaks to the structure.

When I worked in technology, there was often an assumption from those on the outside that I was technical and knew how the coding worked. But it wasn't like that. Yes, I worked with technical people and sought their advice, but my role was to bring it together and deliver the project on time, to budget and to the required scope and quality.

Equally, there were other people within the same department who had absolutely no involvement in delivering projects. What interested them was launching, and when they would be responsible for managing live service of whatever product that project delivered.

Once the new product or service was live, it was their responsibility to keep it live and to ensure customer satisfaction.

On the outside, it may have seemed like one big technology department with everyone involved, but the day-to-day role of those building new things and that of those maintaining existing things could not have been more different.

I knew from early on I did not enjoy the 'maintain' side. I found it dull, repetitive and unsatisfying – almost running to standstill – but others I worked with loved it. I've always loved the energy of making new things, the variables and the buzz of getting something into the market, but others I worked with found this slow, full of unpredictability and not exciting enough.

Action 2N

As you're looking to understand what it is you'll offer your customers, consider if this dynamic applies to you.

- *Will you build something for them or maintain something?*
- *How does this relate to your experiences to date?*
- *Are there any examples of roles you've particularly enjoyed or not enjoyed that you can use as you consider the position of your business?*

Rethinking your experience

One way or another, you'll have been through a lot, even if it doesn't feel that way. Think about *all* of your professional experience beyond the roles and what you see on the surface. Consider how you can use what you've learned and achieved to propel yourself forward to be seen as an authority by your new customers.

Going back to 1999, my first real-life insight into business was at McDonald's, with the job title of Crew Member. At the time, I saw no value in this beyond the financial compensation I received in exchange for my Saturdays. On reflection, I got real-life insight into how a business:

- implements and utilizes efficient, scalable processes
- effectively uses a just-in-time supply chain model
- uses technology to ensure quality and consistency of product
- successfully uses a franchise model
- uses customer feedback to improve its offering

I also saw first-hand how managers work on performance improvements, teamwork, recruitment, staff rota challenges and staff attitudes towards their role – including people like me who were there to earn some money whilst studying, those who had little ambition and couldn't wait for their shift to end and those who were driven and wanted to grow within the company.

Action 20

Draw a matrix and capture your role, 'people', 'process', 'technology' and what you liked and didn't like for each role you've had over the years. This may include multiple roles, projects or partial roles such as committee memberships within the same company on separate lines. Think about what old skills gained during these roles may be useful in your new business. Consider the following.

People

- *Who did you respect?*
- *What can you learn from them?*
- *Who did you not respect?*
- *What can you learn from them? Sometimes this is more than from those you respect.*
- *Were the right people in place to manage others and ensure processes and technology were used to best effect?*
- *Are there any examples you can learn from where others were setting up a team, function or even a start-up business?*

Processes

- *What processes did the company use?*
- *Did they work?*
- *How could they have been improved?*
- *Were there any alternatives to completely change the ways of working?*
- *Were processes embedded and mandated or did people do their own thing?*

Technology

- *What technology did the company have?*
- *Was it appropriate to support its people and processes?*
- *Did it invest in technology?*
- *If so, did it train people and change processes in order to make the most of it?*
- *If not, what impact did this have on staff having to perform manual, repetitive processes?*

Thinking through these factors will increase your understanding of how the businesses and the roles you've held worked, and how decisions made by management have an impact – both positive and negative – on staff and customers.

When you're a business owner, you'll need to think all of this through – and more. Thinking of your own experience will give you clarity of what – and, as importantly, what *not* – to do when the time comes to shape then create your business.

Accepting sacrifices

The ambition of having a successful business and work–life balance is possible in the longer term, but it's most likely that first you'll need to build the foundations by putting in the hard hours to create and grow your business. This is especially true if you're completing the pre-launch steps in conjunction with your role as an employee or carer.

In the early days, you may need to work long, lonely hours with seemingly nothing to show for it and nobody paying attention, and it can be hard to keep morale high. It's almost certain that at one point you'll get the fear and want to give up.

Depending on the nature of your proposed business, the pre-launch requirements will vary in terms of time, money and energy needed. You'll need to keep this in mind and, before signing off your business case, consider this in relation to what we covered in Phase 0 generally, but specifically in terms of 'Making headspace' and 'The personal factor' from the INPUTS Framework.

Also, in the longer term, will the business give you the lifestyle you're looking for? If it will always require unsociable hours or long periods away from home, consider if this is going to be sustainable.

In Step 3: Trial we'll cover real-world experience for your proposed business, but before getting that far, consider what you'll need to give up if you're to go ahead with your proposal – and, put simply, if you're up for it.

Action 2P

Think through what sacrifices you'll need to make to get your business off the ground.

- *Are you willing to accept them?*

Training options

If you're considering retraining before becoming your own boss, look to understand exactly what you'll achieve from it.

If it's regulatory before you can start the business, that's one thing, but if you're looking purely to get another badge on your blazer, consider what value your customers will place on this. Will it make the difference between them buying from you or a competitor?

Consider the investment, especially if it's significant, and what you could do with that time or money as an alternative. You may be wasting your resources on something when you would be better spending them on physically growing your business.

Having said that, if you do feel strongly that something will be beneficial to you or your business, don't feel bad about investing in yourself. You have to be comfortable if you're to make it a success.

Before starting my own business, I read several business books to develop my understanding and confidence. The value this gave me was greater than any training course or qualification I could have gained at that time. In more recent years I've listened to a lot of business-related podcasts. Some of these have been wide-ranging and very different from what I do, but those are often the interesting ones where I can cross-pollinate and create something of value.

Getting real-world examples from those who have experienced things that I can compare to my own experience, or potential future experience, has been key to my growth and self-confidence.

Action 2Q

Evaluate the pros and cons of formal training before investing in it. Whatever your preferred medium of receiving information, consider what hints and tips you can receive from others. Be creative, and look for trends or approaches from a variety of sectors, industries and markets for inspiration.

Successful case studies

In 'Exploring all ideas' in Step 1: Find, I mentioned that whatever it is you choose to do, the probability is that somebody somewhere has made a success of it previously.

This should give you inspiration and confidence that, if your sweet spot is the same and your INPUTS business case justifies the investment, you can do it too. It also gives you a body of information and lessons learned to craft your own journey.

Finding successful case studies and examples will give you the insight into what steps others have taken, what they got right and what they got wrong. If you review several case studies, you may pinpoint trends of how they got ahead, or even where they failed and what they changed to get back on track.

Tech entrepreneur Paul Hulligan told me about a competitor in the USA and the impact it's had on his business.

It has been operating for years, creating a successful lifestyle business offering similar services as my start-up. I am not scared that it might steal my customers; it inspires me. It's helped me realize I can make this work, people will pay for this regularly. I also point to it in investor meetings by stating, 'look, this can work!'

Action 2R

Find examples of those who have been successful in the niche you're proposing. Look at the 'about us' section on their website. For people, if they're high-profile and have a Wikipedia page, review the 'early career' section. This will often give significant insight into the business and personal journey, and how they made it happen. Consider how you can follow a similar path.

Getting to know the tribe

Looking beyond case studies, there is an opportunity for you to get to know the people out there with similar interests, and often those who have been there and done it before – the tribe.

As part of your research, getting to know the tribe will empower you to decide if this is something you want to be a part of longer term.

Regardless of where you live, you can connect to people in the tribe online and exchange experiences and ideas through a medium like a Facebook group. This is a huge opportunity that simply didn't exist a generation ago.

Especially if you live in a city, the tribe may organize events online and meet in person. A handy place to find out about events that may interest you is meetup.com, which will give you access to local groups covering just about everything you can think of. Some groups are free; others charge. If a group doesn't exist for what you want, for a fee you can start one and see who else joins. You can also find out what is going on via local community sites or, indeed, a web search.

The benefits of this can be subtle. From the embryonic stage of the life of this book and the business I've created around it, just turning up and talking to people about my plans clarified and developed my thinking.

Looking back, my early experiences of networking events were almost always negative. In a corporate environment, where you're expected to be there, smile and talk to people about stuff you're paid to do, it always felt a bit awkward and forced – a bit like inviting a family member to a wedding because you're obliged to do so, rather than because you want to. They turn up because they are expected to, but you both know they'd rather be somewhere else.

Voluntary events like these, however – where people are there purely because they want to be – couldn't feel more different. There is an energy in the room and people are there to talk about stuff they love doing.

It's win–win. If you don't enjoy it, you'll learn you need to re-think – be it slightly or significantly. If you do enjoy it, on the other hand, you'll know you can dig deeper, get more involved and make *the* tribe *your* tribe.

Action 2S

Research meetup.com and see if there are any events locally, or online, you can attend that may pique your interest. Look at LinkedIn groups and Facebook groups for the same reason. Once you've found them, join and get involved.

Outsourcing

We touched on outsourcing in 'The useful factor' of the INPUTS Framework, then when looking at 'Personality types' and 'Adaptive skills', so let's consider it in more detail.

Outsourcing of activities has become more and more common in business since the millennium. At its simplest definition, this is getting an external party to do something your business requires.

There can be many drivers for outsourcing. Sometimes it's cheaper than doing things yourself. Sometimes it can be quicker. Sometimes you can't deliver the same quality. Sometimes it can simply allow you to focus on other, more strategic tasks.

Years ago, when DIY needed to be done at home, I tried to do most things myself. I was terrible at it. I didn't enjoy it or take much satisfaction from completing the task. It was a relief when it was finished.

Then I realized this was a false economy. By doing everything myself, I was inefficient. I spent so much time doing something poorly that an expert could have done quickly and to a higher standard. I also spent a considerable amount of time doing the really basic stuff. This resulted in me not having the time to focus on my skills and interests to improve my offering.

When it came to building and finishing our extension, apart from setting the requirements and helping my wife decide on the finish, I didn't lift a finger. Yet, I didn't feel bad about this and, looking at the bigger picture, nor did it cost me financially.

Focusing instead on my own skill set in project management consulting, I was able to earn more than I had to pay the builders and decorators. Not working long evenings painting or laying a floor in addition to the day job meant I was fresh and able to deliver for my client in the daytime, which may have made the difference when the client considered extending my contract.

It isn't just financial implications, as the builders were able to complete the work quicker and to a higher quality than I would have done, and I didn't have the frustration or regret of doing something I didn't enjoy.

Outsourcing is not just for business tasks, either. I've used a personal example here, and the techniques we covered in 'Making headspace' absolutely apply throughout your business journey. All of your time is precious.

In terms of approach, many business tasks can now be outsourced using an online marketplace for freelance services to people anywhere in the world who become part of your virtual team.

When I first started uploading videos to promote myself online, I used these marketplaces to find a freelancer to add subtitles. I didn't have a clue how to do this, but I found a professional who did it to a high standard and delivered it quickly at an acceptable price.

Outsourcing tasks you're not good at, don't enjoy or don't need to do will allow you to focus your energy where you can add real value and, as a result, enable you to build a better business.

Action 2T

Make a list of the tasks you expect to complete within your business, and score them between 1 and 5 (low to high) based on 'time', 'money', 'quality' and 'regret'. These four numbers can then be multiplied to size it and then used to consider what you should outsource. Once you've completed this, you can add the detail to your business case prioritized as a high, medium or low requirement (per 'The useful factor'). Also, consider how you can outsource tasks or grow a virtual team using technology.

Starting a partnership

Starting a partnership with one or more people can be an excellent way to pool resources, split the key roles that every business needs and launch a bigger business quickly. However, it also reduces your control and requires a degree of trust that your business partner(s) will do what they say they're going to do.

Whilst almost everything covered in this book remains valid in a partnership scenario, it's also worth considering the additional variables a multi-person business brings.

Agri-food innovator Ryan Edwards explained to me why he chose to start a partnership, and the benefits this has had.

> *I realized that continuing alone was fine, but I could go further and deeper with trusted partners due to the additional perspectives and wider network they bring. It's like the African proverb, 'If you want to go fast, go alone. If you want to go far, go together.'*
>
> *We were good friends for five years before we went into business together, initially with me as his boss in our first*

start-up and now as equal partners in our second. Everyone told us it would be a huge mistake, but it's been hugely rewarding instead. It's worked because we share the same values and vision for the business.

Action 2U

Understand as much as you can about your proposed partner(s) and trust your instincts before proceeding. Consider the following.

Practical considerations

- *What will you bring to the table?*
- *What will they bring to the table?*
- *Are all roles clearly defined?*
- *How complementary are your skills?*
- *What skills gaps will there still be, and how will you fill them?*
- *Who will have the final say on strategy?*
- *How will you be accountable to each other?*
- *How is equity to be split?*
- *Will the equity vary over time?*

Suitability considerations

- *Is their vision for the business the same as yours, including the exit plan?*
- *How similar are your values?*
- *What are their financial needs?*
- *How do their financial needs compare to yours?*
- *How well do you know them?*
- *Have you worked with them before, or do you only know them in a social setting?*
- *How similar is your experience?*
- *What history do they have of committing to long-term projects?*

Joining an existing business or a start-up

Another option is to join an existing business or a start-up, not as an employee but as a co-owner or director.

Compared to starting a partnership, the variable here is that there are likely to be more stakeholders involved, and the processes, systems and offering may already be in place. You may not be needed full-time, and it may be that your input is recurring or *ad hoc*. You may also not receive remuneration in the traditional sense, rather shares or other financial incentives linked to the success of the business. The needs of every business are different.

Whatever the set-up, it's worth considering the same questions covered above in 'Starting a partnership'. How equity may vary over time is especially valid if joining an active business as it's unlikely it will offer significant equity until you've added value and shown commitment over a period of time.

Parenting coach Elaine Halligan explains how she joined an existing business.

> *I initially came on board as a trainee facilitator. Then a curious series of events occurred; Melissa Hood, the founder, decided she wanted to return home to Australia. But the business was thriving in London and through a variety of circumstances her then business partner decided not to continue. So, I was invited to step in and become a co-owner and director. That was 11 years ago, and I've never looked back.*

> *I remember at the time feeling as though I couldn't do it. I was filled with imposter syndrome. I loved what the business stood for, but I never imagined myself as an entrepreneur and business owner.*

> *I felt overwhelmed, scared and consumed with self-doubt. I had no idea what it involved. And we had, what seemed at the time, a really challenging position with me running a business in London and Melissa based in Australia. We laugh about it now, because it means we can support our global clients 24/7. With such a large time difference one of us is almost always online, and it's worked.*

I think this is a great example of what can be done, not just for a partnership, but for how a business can operate around the sun, supporting customers around the world.

Fear and doubt are natural, but you have to quantify them, and Melissa must have believed the business would be in good hands with Elaine, or she wouldn't have asked in the first place.

If an opportunity like this comes to you, don't be too hasty in rejecting it. Consider the pros and cons for you, and remember: if someone has asked you, they must believe you can do it.

Action 2V

Consider in what scenarios joining an existing business or a start-up would be a viable option for you – if any. Make a list of the type of businesses you'd consider joining, and how you see yourself adding value. If there is a business that could be the right fit, make contact with it.

Steering Meeting 2: Go ahead to Step 3: Trial, or return to Step 1: Find

Once you've understood your proposal in terms of the business itself, why the business could work for you, those already in the market and your options for getting into that market, it'll be time for Steering Meeting 2.

The key output from this meeting will be to sign off your draft business case to take it into Step 3: Trial. If you're looking to take forward more than one proposal, you may choose to hold a separate meeting for each.

As before, capture a key milestone on your plan for when you think you'll be confident to understand enough and make the right decision. Then, schedule the meeting with your SteerCo.

Consider which of the sub-steps we've covered here can be used to justify your proposal – or not, as the case may be – and add them as agenda items. You may wish to touch on all of them, and also take along an early draft of your INPUTS business case.

If you're happy that your proposal justifies more of your attention and that you should analyse it in the real world, then your decision should be to sign it off, pass through the gate and move on to Step 3: Trial. If so, congratulations!

On the other hand, if your bids didn't stand up to the scrutiny you gave them, your next step is to return to Step 1: Find. There are bright sides to this – as I say frequently, it's better to know now, but also through the deep analysis of Step 2: Understand, you may have a clearer idea of what may work for you. You may already have found it.

Whether your next step is forward or back, it's a fantastic achievement to have got this far.

Retrospective

As you reach the end of this step you should now understand your proposed investment and how it may fit with your circumstances.

Initially, we looked at the *business environment* you'll enter by considering the tools, processes and strategic options available to understand and develop your proposed business.

Next, we looked at *your own motivations* as to why you're proposing this business, and how you can make the business work for you.

We then considered what you can *learn from others* who have already made an impact in this market – both for you to learn from and collaborate with.

At the end of this step we covered Steering Meeting 2, where the strategic decision is whether to go ahead to Step 3: Trial or return to Step 1: Find.

This should have been tough, and if it was, you'll receive the benefits later, once you launch your business.

Let's now move on to look at trialling your proposed business in the real world.

Step 3:
Trial

The scope

In the final step of Phase 1, we cover how a business uses a pilot to validate its products and services, and how this vital step can avoid tears, pain and regret. This is where the theory stops, and the action starts.

Not everything will work, but that's normal. Whilst in Step 3: Trial, your investment is minimal and easy to adapt, and failure should be seen positively. Knowing now will save you significant pain further down the line, and once you get it right, you can confidently make plans to go further.

At the end of this step we cover your third Steering Meeting. This is the biggest milestone of your entire project, where you'll review your completed INPUTS business case and where you'll decide whether to go ahead with your business proposal.

Let's start trialling!

The pilot

In a corporate project, there comes a time when all the theory has to stop, and an offering has to be put in front of real people to see how it fares. This is often called a pilot. There are many benefits to this, including proving that the technology works as planned and receiving customer feedback.

Your trial is slightly different. Yes, you want to prove there's a market to make sales, and that's one of the six INPUTS factors you'll need to approve in your business case. The rest, however, is about proving or disproving your thinking and that your understanding of what you'll be getting into matches the reality.

Pilots are designed to be low-risk. They are low-volume, time-limited and, if sold physically, limited in their geographical reach to a small number of locations (or even a single one). In a corporate setting, they are often not advertised. Guidelines will be agreed in advance of what constitutes success or failure.

You learn best through experience, and this is the last opportunity for you to fail fast before committing to your business investment.

Action 3A

Consider how you'll deliver a pilot.

- *What will you offer?*
- *How will you get it to market?*
- *How long will you make it available for?*
- *What success criteria will you work to?*

Getting comfortable with feeling uncomfortable

In 'Openness to change' in Pre-step 1: The SORTED Framework, I asked whether you had 'imposter syndrome' – where you feel you won't fit in or have enough to succeed. This is very common and is at risk of happening as you begin your trial and start talking about your business publicly.

I spoke with psychologist and entrepreneur Lynda Holt about this. Lynda explains.

> *When you put your own stuff out there, it can be scary. You can feel like an imposter. However, if you're not feeling out of your depth and a little uncomfortable, then I don't believe you're growing.*

> *Get comfortable with feeling uncomfortable. You need a balance, and not to take it too far, but constantly pushing your own boundaries will help you grow, and it becomes a habit. You can easily get into a habit of stretch, and then staying in the habit of looking for something new to stay in a growth mindset.*

Your brain prioritizes information that is essential for survival. It will bring things that are different or threatening into your conscious awareness. By being regularly uncomfortable you train your brain to operate better in uncertainty – or to process new information in a way that is more conducive to learning. Eventually, a new neural pathway forms which becomes your new default.

The benefit of this cannot be overstated, and I chose to place this at the start of Step 3: Trial because it's about 'little and often' rather than a single one-off exercise.

When I decided to put a video up on YouTube and LinkedIn introducing this book and asking for contributors, I felt deeply uncomfortable and exposed. It wasn't published live – I could have recorded 100 takes if necessary, and nobody was asking me awkward questions – but I knew people would see it and it would make the product, this book, better. The vast majority of the contributors to this book, including Lynda via an introduction, came to me as a result of the discomfort of planning, recording and posting that video.

Action 3B

Think about what your business needs from you that you're uncomfortable doing. It could be the sales process, for example.

- *What initial steps can you take to begin growing and get used to feeling uncomfortable?*
- *How can you build regular growth into your routine to get into a habit of stretch?*

Minimum viable product

Before committing to your business, you need to know that what you plan to offer will strike a chord with your core customer, and that they will see the same value as you.

A typical way to trial your offering is to develop a minimum viable product (MVP). This is an early version of a product (which, of course, includes services) that has just enough features to work for early customers.

The temptation is always to not launch something until it's perfect, but that approach brings multiple risks. For a start, what if you develop a perfect product nobody wants? What if your cash runs out before you've generated enough – or even any – revenue?

The MVP will prove or disprove your assumptions without having had a long incubation period or development process where you may be wasting time, money and energy on something your core customer won't value, or you won't enjoy delivering.

At the earliest opportunity, release your MVP to test your proposal on real people. Try multiple channels to market (if your product allows that) and vary your pricing. The real-world feedback you gather will be invaluable in giving you a sense of what works and what doesn't. It will then enable you to define your next steps, and ultimately give you confidence in the viability of your business case and plan.

Action 3C

Consider all the products, services or features you'd ideally have in your business. Capture the core elements you can try as part of an MVP, and what can wait. Decide how and when you'll market your MVP.

- *How will you validate it?*
- *How will this support decision-making going forward?*

Choosing a business name

A bit like naming your project at the start of Step 1: Find, before going public with your trial it's time to choose a name for your business.

Brand transformation expert Vicki Young explains why you shouldn't allow this decision to delay your progress.

> *You can spend so long procrastinating about a name or logo when you're right in the beginning stages. You could use this time to get on with your business. Call it something and be willing to change it later, if it's justified. Companies change names all the time. They merge, they acquire. A name does inform the brand, but not to the level people may fear. It's the brand as a whole that people build a connection with, not just the name.*

This isn't necessarily the time to register the business (covered later in 'Making it real' in Step 4: Undertake), but check regulations locally. Some geographies require registration before conducting any business, as well as business insurance.

If you ever do need to change a name, it can be done legally, or you could use a 'trading name' for your day-to-day business which is different from the registered company name. If considering using a trading name, again check regulations locally.

To avoid the need for name changes, there are some considerations to ensure you make an appropriate choice.

- Avoid anything that is too common, or even your core customer may not be able to find you online.

- Avoid a name that is difficult to say or spell. You want to stand out, but at the same time it needs to be relatable. It can be easy to be too clever and just confuse people.
- Ensure your name doesn't hold you back. Names that include a geographic location can lead to people considering they don't belong beyond the specified place in the name. There are exceptions to this rule, but unless your reach will never expand beyond that place and you never intend to move, it might not be worth the risk.
- Consider a personal brand – your own name with, perhaps, your specialism added. It's easy to hide behind an anonymous company name but if you're likely to be the face of your company, why not put yourself out there? That's what I've done, and from my own experience, it has certainly given strong engagement. People work with and buy into people.

Before settling on a name, check that the website domain is available. Ideally, this will be a '.com', the default domain name extension, but if it's not available, consider if you can tweak the web address and still make it work for your company. A non-'.com' address isn't the end of the world; I settled with www.robkerr.co.uk and it's perfectly simple and easy for people to find.

In addition to having a strong web address, being able to use the name clearly and consistently is highly advantageous. There are tools, such as www.namecheckr.com, that allow you to check the availability of a name across many web domains and social media sites without trawling through them individually.

Action 3D

Make a list of potential names and test them on a relevant audience, perhaps your SteerCo. Check if the web address is available in '.com' and, if so, buy it (or even multiple domain name extensions). Register all main social media accounts in the same clear and consistent name. Register the business name if local regulations require this.

Real-world experience

Before starting his independent career, tech entrepreneur Paul Hulligan found a group on meetup.com who met at a café within the British Film Institute (BFI) in London on a monthly basis to have coffee and talk about documentary films.

This was one of several meetup groups he had explored whilst in employment after moving to London, which he did in order to find his tribe and learn with a view to becoming a freelance film person. Paul explains.

> *I focused on documentary film groups because I loved the medium, and wanted to make sure if I headed in a new direction it's a direction I'm really passionate and excited about. In the back of my mind, I was figuring out what I could do in that world, and learning if I could skill myself up to be a freelance filmmaker.*

Paul enjoyed it and started going regularly. He asked to get involved to help run the meetup, and also to make it bigger, including screening events – so he could meet even more people in the industry.

The group was growing, and he helped formalize the management, bringing in others who attended regularly with complementary skill sets. The London Documentary Network was founded, as a Community Interest Company (CIC) – an official registered company type in the UK run as a not-for-profit social enterprise, with Paul as one of five co-founders.

When running the meetups, Paul noticed a similar theme coming out of them. He explains.

> *Everyone wanted to make a film but never had the time or always had excuses as to why it hadn't happened, so I suggested we start a competition. The team put their heads together, and 'Doc in a Day' was the result. It's a competition where participants are put into teams, given a topic and create a short documentary film over a single weekend. There is a screening event and independent judging held shortly afterwards. It has brought structure, deadlines, teamwork, opportunities to learn and lots of fun to the group.*

Through this low-risk trial, with the only significant investment being his time, Paul got to know and understand his tribe, to learn about starting a company, running events, leading and adding value. He also got to develop his filmmaking skills, grew his experience, made great connections within the industry and met his future business partner.

Another example is optimist and entrepreneur Sam Halligan, who shares the origins of his business.

> I was always interested in cars, so I started by buying a 1970s Fiat 500 from auction and refurbishing it. I then replicated this, buying two more Fiats from the source in Italy. On reflection, it was a lot of work for not a lot of reward, but it was a learning curve, and I enjoyed it.
>
> As the Fiats hadn't been as successful as I wanted, I tweaked the model. I decided to buy a Range Rover from Barcelona. I advertised it and got a call asking if I could ship it to Dubai. I said 'of course' – I didn't have a clue how to do it. The process was backwards and terrifying, but addictive at the same time. I sold the car for twice what I bought it for.
>
> Then other markets appeared, and I started getting clients in North America. It took 18 months to get to that stage. I'd done the Fiats, learned some lessons, did a lot of research then came out with a solution that worked: buying the right cars from Europe, selling them out of Europe from the UK. I would identify the client needs, source the cars, then pitch them to the right market. There's a big following in the USA for English cars that are left-hand drive, for example.

Your situation might be very different from Paul's or Sam's, but in both circumstances the ingredients of what makes a valuable trial are there: offering real-world experience, validating thinking and being part-time, low-risk and built on solid foundations.

Action 3E

- *How can you seek – or, if they don't exist, create – oppor-tunities that'll provide both clarity and experience before finalizing your proposal and making your decision?*

Range of trial options

There is no one-size-fits-all to trialling being your own boss, and depending on your personal and professional circumstances you'll need to find a solution that works for you. This is by no means exhaustive, but below are some of your options.

Volunteering. This will give you hands-on, real-world experience of what it's like to work in a certain field, with low risk. Whatever you agree with the company or group you volunteer with, the main thing you'll be committing is your time.

Adult internship. It's common to think that internships are just for those at entry level in their career, but that isn't the case. Taking an adult internship, normally one to three months in length and unpaid, will allow you to grow your network and understand the structure of a business similar to the one you may wish to create.

Side-hustle. A side-hustle is work alongside your day job. It's often freelance or piecework in nature. As it runs parallel to your day job and doesn't interfere with it, a side-hustle can be considered a low-risk way of trialling your ideas. Once in a side-hustle, you can assess the impact you're having and extrapolate the results if you were to commit more to it.

Be aware if going down this route not to be in breach of your contract with your employer. Read the contracts you've signed and always keep to your legal obligations. If you're not currently permitted to operate a side-hustle, once you understand your legal position and you can pitch that you won't be in direct competition with your employer, be transparent and tell them about your plans. They may ask you to sign new documents, and they may even be supportive. It's also worth discussing with an accountant to ensure you remain tax-compliant.

Permanent job. It may sound counter-intuitive to take a new permanent job if you wish to become your own boss, but it isn't always so. I was employed as a consultant long before I decided to undertake a role under my own banner, and agri-food innovator Ryan Edwards had his first taste of entrepreneurship running a start-up for somebody else.

Just starting. Sometimes it doesn't need a label, and your trial is just about starting. When optimist and entrepreneur Sam Halligan bought a Fiat 500 at auction he had no idea it would lead to sourcing cars in Italy, Spain and beyond and selling them worldwide.

An initial opportunity may not be perfect; it may come with a limited financial return and the location or working hours may not be ideal, but you have to balance this against the benefit you'll get from it and understand that it isn't permanent.

Action 3F

Consider what trial option will work best for you.

- *How and when will you make a start?*

Get those milestones added to your plan.

Your elevator pitch

Creating, rehearsing and delivering an elevator pitch will give you clarity on your message. A clear, narrow focus for your pitch will also ensure a clear, narrow focus for your business.

Getting this right during Step 3: Trial can help prove the premise behind your proposed business, or provide vital feedback to enable you to improve it early on.

An elevator pitch will allow you to share your message with others to get their attention, and create the opportunity for them to buy into you and your business. They may become early advocates, suppliers or even customers.

I asked communications expert Sara Price what makes a good elevator pitch. Sara defined two approaches, depending on the environment. Let's look at them separately.

At a networking event

Imagine you've just been introduced to somebody at an event – a potential client or possible collaborator – and they ask you 'So, what do you do?'

First, avoid being in what I call 'broadcast mode' – all talking and no listening! You're aiming for engagement; you want to have a two-way conversation – an opportunity to learn about them as well as to tell them about you. The best route into that is to leave them space to ask questions and to ask some yourself.

If you launch into a monologue with the aim of telling them absolutely everything about you and your business, you'll overwhelm them. Instead, explain what you do in the most succinct way possible and pique their interest enough to ask more questions.

I asked Sara how she would structure the elevator pitch in that scenario.

When someone asks me what I do, I answer in two parts – the problem I solve, and how I solve it. Then I ask them about what they do. If what I do is intriguing or relevant to them, they'll ask me for more information. If not, I haven't wasted their time with reams of explanation.

I like this approach. As soon as someone engages in conversation you have permission to say more. Unlike what often happens, they won't be listening because it's polite to do so, but because they want to hear more.

Introductory remarks at a speaking event

You have more time when you're introducing yourself and your work as a speaker. But you also need to capture and hold your audience's attention. So, you want to inspire them with the breadth and scale of the vision and invite them to join you on your journey.

For example, I would say something like 'Imagine a world in which every business is led with purpose, where every entrepreneur knows that they can make money and make a difference and where all parts of our society work together towards one common aim: to create positive change in the world. That's the world I envisage. And through my business, that's the world I am trying to create. This is how I'm doing it...'

Although your audience in this scenario isn't likely to respond outwardly, it gets them thinking and engages them. Whilst they're listening they can imagine where they see themselves being involved in delivering your vision. It also gives them a natural follow-up if they choose to engage with you after the speech.

Action 3G

Create your elevator pitch for both the networking event and speaking event scenarios.

- *How can you get someone's attention as succinctly as possible?*
- *How can you get their engagement and their buy-in to your vision?*
- *What will your follow-up be, and when will be the right moment to talk about selling?*

Creating opportunities

Within 'Pre-step 1: The SORTED Framework' we looked at 'Tenacity', and how seeing an opportunity that doesn't appear to exist can benefit your business. Not all opportunities are obvious, and sometimes you need to create them.

If you've identified somewhere you'd like to work or someone you'd like to work with, approach them armed with your elevator pitch and your proposal for your business. Clearly set out how they fit into your vision and what's in it for them, and see what they say.

Tech entrepreneur Paul Hulligan saw the value in getting the founder and former CEO of a larger rival onto his advisory board (what we're labelling as the SteerCo). Unsolicited, Paul and his business partner spent significant effort creating a film for this CEO's new business and sent it to him. Surprised and delighted with the gift, the CEO was happy to join the advisory board as Paul wanted, and became part of his team. Paul explains his strategy.

I didn't get the former CEO on board because I asked; it was how I asked. If I had simply sent him an email it's likely he wouldn't have even replied. Instead, I identified the level of importance and adjusted the effort I put into asking accordingly, and achieved the desired result.

Businesses are run by people, and people like to feel valued. If you value what someone else does, and think this can benefit you, then find a way of letting them know about it for your mutual benefit.

Action 3H

Develop a plan for how you can start to become known, liked and trusted in the niche and wider industry you're proposing to join. Decide the outcomes you want to achieve from each approach.

Adapting to those who find value

The chances are you'll also appeal to other types of customers beyond the core customer you identified in Step 2: Understand, or customers will want something different than what you plan to offer.

As soon as you go public, you'll find that people will approach you with ideas or suggestions of what might work better for you – and for them.

There is a fine balance of who you listen to here. Some ideas will be brilliant and progress your business, offering something better than you'd ever intended to a more appropriate audience. Others will simply hold you back, divert you away from what you intended to do and potentially reduce your appeal to the majority of your audience.

As long as you don't compromise on your values, there is no problem with updating your purpose, mission and vision statements and developing your offering.

It's also possible to update your core customer or add criteria to them based on the feedback you receive from the market. There is only so much planning you can do, and the real world often makes things much clearer. The key point is that you remain comfortable with any amendments you make, and your message remains consistent.

As we touched on in 'Pivot' in Step 1: Find, when planning her business, home cooking educator Dani Mosley initially planned to hold workshops for parents, showing them how to rustle up a healthy family meal in under 40 minutes. But it didn't work out like that. Dani explains.

> To prove that I could teach and knowing that there was a dearth of good after-school clubs, I started a cooking class for 8–10-year-old children at my daughter's primary. It sold out overnight and I got a real buzz out of it. I realized they are the people I need to inspire.
>
> That is where the market is; parents want their children to know how to cook properly, to understand and be passionate about quality food. Children have the time, which often the parents don't, and I realized this is how I could make a difference for the next generation. A year later, I have a long waiting list.

Similarly, authority on introversion Joanna Rawbone planned to launch new services to help women over 50 who are introverts thrive. She started running webinars for that exact market; however, her audience quickly evolved. Joanna explains.

> Attendees asked if a friend could join who didn't quite fit the age group, and then others asked if male relatives could join, saying they really needed to hear this. The niche started very narrow and then broadened out into all introverts who are ready to step up. I realized I was on to something, and Flourishing Introverts was launched.

Making their ideas public early on helped both Dani and Joanna adapt their planned services to a different audience, and in both cases they were happy with the pivot from their initial plan. The outcome was them offering more value to their audience.

If you aren't happy with a suggestion either because you don't think it will work or because that isn't the direction you want to go in, it's your business and you can politely decline.

Either way, feedback from your audience will always be an opportunity to make your offering stronger.

Action 31

Develop a process for capturing and considering amendments to your offering based on customer feedback.

- *How can you remain consistent with what you want to deliver, whilst implementing changes you see as beneficial to your business?*
- *How will you assess the value an amendment can make to your customers?*
- *How will this impact the scope of your appeal to a wider or more appropriate market?*

Responding to disappointment

What happens if your trial doesn't go to plan and you realize your idea either won't work or isn't for you?

The first step is to think positively, just like when I said to look on the bright side if your BIDS candidates didn't stand up to scrutiny at Steering Meeting 2. It's much better to find out at any point during Phase 1 rather than when you've used your life savings or spent years of unfulfilled commitment for something that was never going to work.

Consider if your sweet spot is wrong, or if one (or more) of the INPUTS factors are significantly out of kilter with your expectations.

Before going back to the drawing board, however, if your core customer wasn't interested, find out the reasons why. Was your message clear enough? Were you offering the right product or service to the right audience?

Also, consider the scale of the trial and how this will correlate to running the business going forward. What percentage of the target market do you need to turn into leads? What percentage of leads do you need to turn into customers?

If you get to Step 3: Trial before deciding not to proceed and there genuinely is no mitigation, I suggest completing the business case and discussing it with your SteerCo to evaluate what went wrong, get their feedback and work out your next steps. Consider what you liked and what you didn't like, because the right answer is out there somewhere.

Remember, think positive!

Action 3J

Explore the reasons why your trial didn't go to plan, and how you can proactively respond.

- *Are there some amendments you can make to your offering, your messaging or your audience?*
- *Is there a further trial you can do before writing off your proposal?*

If you don't proceed, consider your next steps, and which sub-step of the process you should revert to.

The cutover

In software projects, there is a time when an old product (or version) is swapped for a new one. This is called a 'cutover'.

During your trial, get an understanding of how you'll be able to 'cut over' from your old job to your new one, full-time.

There may be a time of parallel running, as we covered when looking at side-hustles, but that is not sustainable in the longer term in order to maximize the opportunities your new business can offer. Doing this indefinitely could lead to burnout or reduced commitment to both your employer and your own business, which isn't fair on them or you.

If you're working full-time for an employer you could ask to reduce your days or hours to assess how this additional bandwidth benefits your new business. You could also see if they might offer a sabbatical, effectively as an extended trial, which would give you every opportunity to succeed whilst keeping your risk low and your options open.

My circumstances were different as I was already a contractor, but the decision I made to take a sabbatical from client work and focus fully on writing this book and then developing the material to support the business around it was vital in making it happen.

Even if you're not in a side-hustle you'll need to make a decision on when to end your trial. If the timing isn't now, that's fine, but be conscious of when is the right time and build it into your business case. If the time isn't now, that doesn't stop you going through the formality of signing off your business case and capturing the milestone for when you'll start. Otherwise, it risks going on the 'never never' list.

Action 3K

Pick a precise date for when you'll be working on your business full-time and make yourself as accountable as you can to make it happen.

Re-baselining your plan

You may reach this stage and realize the original dates you put in were desperately unrealistic, or even in the past already. In this scenario, you'll need to re-plan and, in project manager speak, re-baseline your plan. To do this, you re-evaluate the project as it stands today.

Look at your progress to date and consider how these tasks compared to your requirements. Were the tasks bigger than you thought? Were any smaller? Were your groupings accurate, and did you choose the right priorities? By comparing the remaining tasks to those completed you should be able to make a new plan, with a new proposed completion date.

Stuff happens, and sometimes things don't go to plan, but I strongly recommend that you set a realistic new baseline, including some contingency, and that you only re-baseline once.

If you re-baseline more than once you risk mentally rejecting your plan and then continuing kicking the can down the road as your energy and focus move on to other things.

If you don't make your dates the second time around, view your plan as late with a red RAG status within your reviews (this is covered in detail in Step 5: Review).

You can re-baseline once at any time in your project, but I suggest doing it when you know your original dates are out of reach and when you have a clear indication of when the right date is. That will give you the best chance of achieving your goals.

As you'd expect, I had a plan for delivering the project that is this book, and looking at it from one point of view you could say it's three years late; but, equally, when I re-baselined I made an absolute commitment to my family and my publisher that I'd get it done once a key client contract ended, and I've kept that commitment.

> ### Action 3L
>
> *Be honest with yourself about your plan. If you need to re-base-line, don't be too hasty on setting a new date for each of your milestones – and make sure you only do it once.*

Steering Meeting 3: Signing off your business case

Make no mistake, it's crunch time. We're at the end of Phase 1 and it's make or break. Where the previous two Steering Meetings were in many cases without significant risk and any mistakes could be easily rectified, this isn't. It's decision time!

In an M&A environment, this is when I would typically work with all teams and the SteerCo – essentially all stakeholders – to present and sign off their plans for delivering the integration.

In a technology environment, this is where you'd have a 'Go/No Go' meeting – like the decision you made at the end of Phase 0, but with much more at stake.

Your task is a combination of the two.

Following the completion of your trial, all six factors within your INPUTS business case document (covered in Phase 0) should be completed in full and presented to all of your stakeholders.

Your SteerCo should stay focused as your initial group, but you may wish to socialize the content with others ahead of the meeting, such as friends, family or your children (if you have them and they're old enough to understand). This will be especially valuable if these people share characteristics with your core customer.

If there is anything you're unhappy with from your trial that you haven't been able to amend and resolve, you'll need to flag it here and work with your SteerCo to either find a solution or accept whether the risk should be accepted. The risk may not have a big impact in a trial situation, but it can easily mushroom into an issue that becomes significant during the next phase.

If you can't find a solution or accept the situation, your only option may be to go back to the drawing board and Step 1: Find. As I've said, if that scenario does take place, it's a success, not a failure. As they used to say where I grew up in Essex, 'Chin up!'

But let's assume that it's a success. You've presented a solid business case and all the criteria have been fulfilled.

- Your nearest and dearest are on-board, having accepted the *impact* on them, and are ready to support you.
- The *numbers* justify the investment and are in line with your personal needs.
- It aligns to your *personal* skills, interests and circumstances, and you're full of energy, ready to start.
- You know who you'll find *useful* to support you and are confident they will.
- You've understood when the *timing* will be right and have committed to the date.
- You're confident the market exists and where you fit in to make the *sales* you need.

If all of the above are true, your SteerCo should sign off your business case. You'll pass through the gate and you'll be ready to make it happen. A great achievement!

Retrospective

The end of Step 3: Trial signifies the end of Phase 1 of your project, and hopefully a hugely exciting journey ahead if you sign off your INPUTS business case at Steering Meeting 3.

We've covered how a business uses a pilot to validate its products and services, and how the clarity gained from this vital step can avoid tears, pain and regret.

We've also covered Steering Meeting 3, the biggest milestone of your entire project.

If you decline your business case at Steering Meeting 3, it's time to breathe a big sigh of relief that you didn't invest in that business proposal.

However, if you sign off your business case, and in doing so decide to go ahead with your proposal, then next is Phase 2. There, you'll find out how to make it happen within Steps 4 and 5 of the FUTURE Method: Undertake and Review.

Let's start making it happen!

Phase 2

Making it happen

Initiating Phase 2

Phase 2 is about making it happen. You've done your analysis and you've considered whether it's right for you from a variety of angles. Now it's all about delivery.

Phase 2 consists of two parts: Steps 4 and 5 of the FUTURE Method. These are as follows.

- Step 4: **U**ndertake the activity, now that you're clear, confident and committed.
- Step 5: **R**eview to check progress against expectations.

Unlike in Phase 1, the steps run in parallel and the outputs of each review you hold may result in changes to the activities you undertake.

It's the early life of your business. You'll be learning every day and there are many variables to consider.

When you've completed the actions in Phase 2, you'll have an established business. How exciting!

After a brief pause to think about that, let's get back to reality and think about your plan.

Plan

Like in Phase 1, each sub-step covered in the following pages is a possible workstream that could form part of your Phase 2 plan. Again, depending on your type of business, some may not be relevant, but the value here is in considering them.

Alongside considering each sub-step in turn, you should have some clarity on the content needed to create this plan from your business case, so you're not starting completely from scratch. This is the point at which to add the detail and commit to getting stuff done at certain dates.

Baselining your plan is vital as there are many more moving parts than in Phase 1. This will stop you from being distracted by other tasks that aren't necessary or could go on to form Phase 3. You may wish to involve your SteerCo in the baselining process.

Unlike in Phase 1, you aren't necessarily working towards a key milestone that would signify the end of the phase. In many respects, the key milestone is when you decide to start.

The cycle around Phase 2 could continue almost indefinitely, so it's worth capturing your priority objectives then baselining your plan as soon as you can.

Consider the duration of your Phase 2 plan. Factor in any lag before starting full-time if you're serving a notice period, for example, or where you have less than 100% of your working time available. Once you do start full-time, I'd suggest at least a six-month plan with several key milestones linked to completion of objectives. You'll also plan reviews to ensure you're on track or taking appropriate action if you're not.

Step 4:
Undertake

The scope

It's difficult to say what the most important step is within the six-step FUTURE Method, as I believe each adds value in its own way, and without one of them it wouldn't work. But if you twisted my arm and made me choose one, this would be it.

To undertake is to make it happen, and regardless of how strong your planning is in Phase 1 (although for your sake I hope it's very strong), the real sink-or-swim will come when you implement your idea and create a business.

We cover a lot of ground here, so like Step 2: Understand it's split into three sections – this time aligned with the definition I gave when splitting requirements into types.

Initially, we look at the *strategic* sub-steps. They are the goals and objectives of what your business plans to achieve, and how you'll achieve it.

Then, starting with 'Brand strategy', we look at the *visible* sub-steps. This is how your business will look and feel.

Finally, starting with 'Working environment', we look at the *personal* sub-steps. This is how the business should facilitate your lifestyle and those included in your impact factor.

Remember, this step works in parallel with Step 5: Review, so I suggest you consider them in tandem before taking any firm action.

Let's start undertaking!

Going live

In a technology environment, the 'Go Live' is when the project becomes a product (even if that product is a service).

It's when it's deployed, and it becomes real. It's when customers notice what has been going on behind the scenes for months or even years. It's when marketing teams will start promoting the product. It often goes from a code name to a branded name and becomes visible to scrutiny by the outside world.

The build-up to Go Live is often the most nervous period for project teams. Despite all the planning and the pilot, there is nothing like going live, and the gap between receiving a 'Go' decision from the SteerCo and 'Day 1' of the launch can be excruciating.

Things can, and often do, go wrong. But there are always solutions. This is where your tenacity will come into play to find those solutions.

It may be that your Day 1 is a little more subdued, but it's still a great step and, most important of all, a start. You and your family should certainly mark the occasion and allow yourself a reward for the work that's gone into getting to this point.

As the start of something new and exciting, this is a great opportunity to shout about it and promote your new business. A lot of goodwill comes from business launches, and with this may come opportunity. People will want to help you succeed if they can.

Action 4A

Decide how you'll launch your business.

- *Will it be a quiet day, or will you launch with a marketing campaign and advertising?*
- *How will you mark the day for you and your family?*
- *How will you use it as an opportunity to publish and receive people's goodwill?*

Committing 100%

Once you've signed off your INPUTS business case, it's time to commit 100% to your venture – and there is no turning back.

Depending on your timing factor, however, there may be a hiatus. You may have, for example, a three-month notice period and may have set your resignation milestone in six months' time, meaning you have nine months left in employment. Being committed 100% to your new business doesn't mean being 100% dedicated to it with your time. If that's the case, use this time to do as much as you can in the background, to start as soon as your window opens (without breaking your employment terms).

While going through the coming sub-steps, consider what you can do and when. Some things, like getting suppliers on board, can be painfully slow and organizing this in a light-touch way when it's not urgent can save a lot of pain and delays when you want to get cracking.

A little reminder – you may be going into something new, but as you're pivoting, this ain't your first rodeo. You'll be delivering a new offering, in a new way and possibly to a new customer base. There may be some learnings as a result, but you know what you're doing, and you have much to offer your core customer. They'll be delighted you made the decision.

Action 4B

If you have a hiatus, work out how much time you realistically have available and plan tasks you can complete in the background accordingly – especially those that have a long lead time or lag.

Making it real

An exciting prospect within the early life of your business is to make it real. This is broken into three separate sub-steps, as below, each with their own action.

Registering the company

Review and carefully consider the name you've chosen and used during Step 3: Trial. Then, once you've settled on a name, get the business registered. There is nothing more real than that! You will then be a business owner and have something tangible to be accountable to. It's the easy bit, but a satisfying milestone.

Being registered isn't just good for your morale. It ensures you look professional to customers, makes it easier to attract and receive investment and often protects you from personal liability for any losses the business makes (but carefully check the business type and local regulations on this final point).

If you're looking to secure start-up investment, however, you may wish to delay registering the business for a short time. Some governments provide generous schemes to encourage investors that often come with a time limit. Therefore, in some circumstances, if you're not planning to actively work on or launch the business immediately, it could be beneficial to wait before registering your company and effectively starting the clock on your eligibility for such schemes.

The options and rules around registering a company will vary depending on where you're based, so I won't go into detail. However, it's worth using a search engine to find guidance on setting up a company and your options to ensure you set up the right type.

Once you've registered it, go to your local government website (Companies House in the UK[1]) where you, or anyone else, will be able to type in your company name and see it in all its glory, with you listed as a company director. It's a sweet feeling!

You may already have a company registered, having considered this in the past. DevSecOps consultant Glenn Wilson registered his company in 2002 – a full 13 years before he did anything with it. This goes to show it's never too late, and there was a long-standing purpose for keeping the company active all those years. It acted as a regular reminder to Glenn of his goal as he filed his annual returns (now known as a 'confirmation statement'), which in the UK is necessary each year for the company to remain active.

Action 4Ci

If you're looking for start-up investment, research local schemes that may be available to you and when it's appropriate to register your company. If you're not looking at investment, get it registered!

Hiring an accountant

Once you're registered, the next step is to hire an accountant (although some accountants also register companies, so this step could be done

---

[1] www.gov.uk/government/organisations/companies-house.

first). Accountants can be seen as an overhead, but not only will they help you remain compliant; they may end up saving you money by offering advice on how to run your business efficiently.

They may also offer other services within their plans, such as business insurance, that you'd otherwise need to buy separately.

When looking to hire an accountant, get personal recommendations from your network (or trusted online reviews) before committing to them and ensure they cover your type of business and industry. Some accountants are generic, but many will cover a specific area. It's this specialist knowledge that will justify your investment in them.

Don't think an accountant needs to be based locally to where you live. My accountant is based 300 miles from me. I've never been to their offices or met them in person, but we have an excellent relationship. Like many, they partner with one of the leading accounting software providers to make my input as pain-free as possible. The alignment of their services to your business should be the driver, rather than physical geography.

Action 4Cii

Find the right accountant for you and hire them.

Setting up a business bank account

The final step, which your new accountant may be able to assist with, is to set up a business bank account.

Much like registering the company, it's an amazing feeling when the company bank card comes through the post with the company name on it that you've chosen.

Setting emotion aside, this looks professional and allows you to keep the business's money away from your own, therefore making your admin easier. Once revenue starts to come in, you'll have clarity on available funds for investments that could grow your business. This can, of course, result in a greater personal gain in future in comparison to taking out the maximum revenue for personal use as soon as money is available. It also means you're absolutely ready to start trading.

Action 4Ciii

Find the right business bank account for you and file your application.

Early priorities

Building on what we touched on when looking at the Phase 2 plan, you won't be able to do everything at once, and therefore will need to decide on the early priorities for your business.

The Pareto Principle (also known as the '80/20 Rule') was developed in the 1950s by Dr Joseph Juran[2] from earlier work by economist Vilfredo Pareto. It states that, for many events, roughly 80% of the results come from 20% of the effort. This absolutely applies to you as you get started.

It can be easy to be overwhelmed with everything that could be done, or to overcomplicate things with funky technology solutions, marketing funnels and more. Much of this won't add the value that the effort would justify and would just be a distraction.

Focus on the basics, and choose your priorities to develop an initial offering that will solve your core customer's problem, start making you visible to them, then start making sales with a business model that is as lean as possible.

From another angle, you may be working on the right thing, but consider the appropriate effort for each task. Perfectionism will lead to tasks taking longer than you planned, often with minimal benefit to justify the additional effort and a downstream impact on your ability to complete the other tasks you've identified as being a priority.

Psychologist and entrepreneur Lynda Holt spoke to me about the risks of not focusing on your priorities. This is particularly pertinent in the early life of your business. Lynda explains.

---

[2] Juran (2020). 'Pareto Principle (80/20 Rule) & Pareto Analysis Guide'. www.juran.com/blog/a-guide-to-the-pareto-principle-80-20-rule-pareto-analysis.

If you try to do too much at the same time, you risk things not getting finished. If things don't get finished, you'll feel unsuccessful and think how hard it is. Your brain then looks for reasons to justify how difficult it all is.

On the other hand, if you tell yourself you need to make three phone calls to make contact with three potential clients and you've got a great offering for them, your brain will focus on completing that one thing.

It's about making it into a positive state and making the right chemistry in your body to do what you need to do, rather than leaving it on default. The default position of the brain is keeping you safe, which is the opposite of growth.

Action 4D

Think through your early priorities and add them to your plan. Consider the following when developing your approach.

- *What do you need to do to start solving your core customer's problem?*
- *How will you become visible to them?*
- *What can you delay?*
- *What can you cancel completely?*
- *How can you make the Pareto Principle work for you and avoid perfectionism?*
- *How can you ensure you're focusing on your priorities and not doing too many tasks at once?*

Long-term goals

When looking at your requirements, some bigger goals will take time to achieve, and it can take the completion of several objectives to get there.

Brand transformation expert Vicki Young focused on a three-year plan as she founded her business, and has continued to iterate using the same approach ever since. Vicki explains.

When I started the business, I had a goal to get into our own office by Year 3. It wasn't a priority initially and would have been a risk until the business had proved an investment like that was justified. I started the business as quickly and lean as I could, based in the living room of the house-share I was living in at the time.

As the business grew, it moved it into a shared office space with friends who were running their own businesses, then by Year 3 I achieved the goal of having our own office. We then moved again, into an office with our own front door.

Each of these investments was appropriate to the business needs at the time, and helped drive it to the next stage. The next step was in mind all the way through, always aiming three years ahead.

Vicki concludes by sharing the benefits of having this long-term view.

It's easy to overestimate where you can get in a year, but also it's easy to underestimate what can be done in three years. It's possible to have a bad year and for something unexpected to push you off-track. Sometimes things go better than planned, sometimes worse, so having sight of the bigger picture will allow you to keep things in perspective and not panic if there is a set-back.

Just like currency markets or share prices, it's easy to look at the daily ups and downs, the drama and headlines within your business. However, when taking a step back and looking at the bigger picture, short-term challenges can often (although not always) become insignificant. It's just part of the way you'll need to plan and be responsive as a business owner.

Maintaining a high-level three-year plan will enable your business to be goal-driven, and always looking ahead.

Action 4E

Write 'Three-Year Plan' on a piece of paper and capture your top five long-term goals to be achieved over the next three years, and the month in which you'd like to achieve them.

> - *What objectives will you need to complete during Phase 2 to ensure these goals remain achievable?*
> - *How will you ensure you don't overestimate what you can achieve in your first year?*
> - *How will you ensure you don't underestimate what you can achieve over a three-year period?*

Building momentum to get started

Getting started is one of the most difficult things you can do, but the key is to start small and build some momentum. At the time I won my first three-month contract it felt like a short period of time, and insecure, but compared to many examples I've seen since it was very secure!

Tech entrepreneur Paul Hulligan explains his experience.

> *I literally took any video job. A contact offered me the chance to make a video for a London council about an art project, for little pay, outdoors in the middle of winter – I jumped on it. Alongside this, I worked part-time for free for a professional film director, which led to paid work. I jumped on these opportunities because it was all about building the portfolio and getting known – which led to better-paid work in the future. I had to prove myself.*

Similarly, digital marketing expert Sophie Southmayd explains how she utilized her social media presence.

> *I had a personal Instagram that I'd used to exhibit my portfolio and build my network when I moved from Canada to London. Later, when I launched my business, I knew my niche was female-owned start-ups, so I put all of my energy into getting known in that community.*

As long as your commitment is negligible, in this scenario it's worth not being too fussy about the opportunity you take. You never know where it will lead, and being under- or over-qualified has much less relevance than in a permanent role. If someone wants a job done and you're up for it, that can often be enough.

My initial contract wasn't perfect – it was more technology-centred than I would have liked – but it was the first step. Equally, Paul's early clients (and fees) may not have been what he was looking for longer term, but it built his portfolio and got him known to the right audience.

Action 4F

Consider what assets you already have, both professional and social, then make a list of ten positive actions you can take to start building momentum.

Asking for help

It may not seem obvious, but people in your sector – even competitors – are often willing to share their knowledge and experience. To get the benefits of this, though, you have to be willing to ask, and to accept help when it's offered.

Communications expert Sara Price shares her experience of this.

I co-founded my first entrepreneurial business following the financial crash of 2008. At a time like that – with fewer clients, looking to spend less money – you would assume that the competition wouldn't be willing to help the 'new kids on the block'. And yet, the amount of support and goodwill that we received from other agency owners within our sector was quite extraordinary. We weren't expecting it, and we were blown away by our experience.

This pattern was repeated when I started my second business. I've enjoyed an incredible amount of support, goodwill, referrals and advocacy from people that would traditionally be regarded as competitors.

This is something I've actively engaged in and benefitted from over the years. Ahead of my transition to contracting, I spoke to several contractors about their experiences and it certainly shaped the decisions I made. It wasn't long after I'd made the leap myself that others started asking me the same questions and I became the person sharing my knowledge. To some extent, that was the catalyst for this book.

Moving on a few years, before I started speaking at events I joined a public speaking group. This was the safe environment that I needed to grow my confidence and learn about the right structure of a speech. I was then ready to stand in front of a live audience. These fantastic people volunteer their time because they have a skill they'd like others to improve.

Action 4G

Decide what gaps in your knowledge or experience would benefit from the insight of others. Work out where you can find them, and who they are. Finally, get in touch with them! You have nothing to lose and could be pleasantly surprised by the response.

Cash-flow is king

What I remember most from my Dad talking about his business is him saying 'cash-flow is king'. Upon growing my own business, the value of this simple statement became clear in running a business well and keeping it sustainable.

Cash comes in; cash goes out. That's business, but often they are not in sync. You may need to pay upfront for some products or services and have a significant lag until you get paid, either due to payment terms with your clients of 30, 60 or even – dare I say – 90 or 180 days (best avoided!).

You may have negotiated favourable payment terms, but the client could pay you late, or you may need to wait for sales not yet achieved before you can recoup your outgoings, with your cash tied up in stock.

Having absolute clarity on your planned cash-flow will not only allow you to keep your head above water in the general cycle; it will also allow you to manage your risk to ensure you're covered for that unexpected downturn which is likely to come at some point.

In 'Long-term goals' above, brand transformation expert Vicki Young stated to not panic when something unexpected knocks you off-track. A proven way to mitigate the impact of this is to ensure you have the cash-flow in place. Vicki explains.

> *I started saving early to have some buffer for cash-flow. My target from very early on was to ensure I could continue to run the studio for three months without any clients. This would enable me to pay the staff and other overheads and give us time to get our ducks in a row with new clients.*
>
> *We've had growth every year, but we did have a bad year where we lost a big client and had too many eggs in one basket. Having the savings in place saved us from needing to talk to the banks, and it's a concept I've continued to use as we've expanded.*

As you get used to managing two sets of finances – those of your business in addition to your personal finances – you should find a balance. Many business owners choose to pay themselves less than they earned as an employee even if there is money available. This is not necessarily to manage day-to-day cash-flow or tax efficiency, but rather to set money aside for investments.

Another risk, although a nice position to be in, is the risk of over-trading. You may be offered what seems like the deal that will make your company, but if you're not careful it could be the one to break your company if your commitments become too big and cash-flow isn't in place to manage it.

There are a lot of variables at play here, so it's worth discussing with your accountant, but always remember: cash-flow is king!

Action 4H

Quantify your buffer cash-flow target and don't commit beyond it.

- *How much money, and when, do you want to set aside for investments?*
- *How will you counter the risk of over-trading?*

You're never 'unemployed'

When you're a business owner, a point to factor in is that you're no longer, ever, 'unemployed'. Even if you don't have any customers, you're a company director working on developing your business, and there's always something to be done.

Consulting companies have something called a 'bench' to term members of the team not currently engaged with a client. These team members are used by the company to deliver internal projects, normally creating or improving intellectual property (IP). Exactly the same principle applies to you.

Not having any customers is not a reason to stay in bed all day or sit watching daytime TV, but is instead clear headspace and a great opportunity to improve your offering, take a training course, develop assets or grow your network.

These could be some of the busiest days you ever have, but at the same time they could be a chance to strike a balance with other aspects of your life.

I wrote a fair chunk of this book whilst we were visiting family in Vietnam. The luxury of working from a laptop means I was able to continue unhindered, including holding free video calls over the internet. It was still work, and I treated it with the same discipline as if I were in my regular work environment. Knowing I was working allowed us to be away for longer, and the downtime I did have was planned in advance. The key point is I didn't consider myself to be on holiday the moment we got on the plane.

Action 4I

Plan for the day you don't have any customers.

- *What will be on your to-do list?*

Consider what tasks you can complete from a different location, whether that is by choice or necessity. Even if your business is normally geography-specific, there are always some tasks that can be done from elsewhere.

Reputation is everything

Back when I was employed, I received an accomplished piece of advice from a senior director. I'd asked him how he'd elevated his career from such a young age. His advice was simple: 'Prove you can provide value to the company, and also to the customer, and you'll always be in demand. It's a rare and fine balance'.

I never forgot that, and I think it applies equally as you start your own business. The only difference is that you'll be providing value to your own company and treating it well.

In terms of providing value to your customers, I think that's fairly simple. If you're realistic, do what you say you'll do and don't over-promise, then you'll likely generate mutually beneficial relationships.

In many scenarios, especially as you're starting, attitude is more important than experience. A customer may not even be interested in what you see as a deficiency as long as you're honest about what you can achieve and by when.

As the world gets more and more connected, negative feedback about your work online is the biggest risk to progress and development, in every industry.

I have always looked to end relationships well. Even in a notice period, I've worked hard up until the last day. I remember being at one company until nearly 7pm on my last day. I almost turned the lights out! These are the things that get remembered.

As you move on, your previous employers effectively become your past customers, and who's to say they, or others within the company, won't become your customers in future?

You may have customers for the long term or for short transactions, but if they leave delighted with the experience and the offering you've provided, you'll always be in demand.

Action 4J

Break down your offering into a number of smaller activities and capture your business's proficiency at each as 'advanced', 'intermediate' or 'novice'. Use this to be honest and realistic with your customers.

> - *How will you ensure you do what you promised, and delight them?*
> - *What seeds can you plant so that they become a repeat customer or share their positive experience with other potential customers?*

Abundance

It may seem counter-intuitive when you're trying to build a business, but the more generous you are, the more you share and the more you give away for free, the more successful you're likely to be.

This doesn't mean being walked over by customers or not valuing your own time. As we saw when looking at 'Competitive differentiators' in Step 2: Understand, that would be a disastrous strategy. Rather, it means that sharing resources that help others – both your audience and other businesses in your sector – can result in a cycle of goodwill, and ultimately benefit your business.

This is an abundance mindset as opposed to a scarcity mindset. Having it will result in people remembering you positively. They'll recommend you to others, and they'll want to work with you, which may result in all sorts of unexpected opportunities. It's also a great way to live your life.

In the digital world ideas and information are so readily available that keeping things to yourself or demanding a fee for small actions will result in nobody talking about you or being willing to do something for you.

If your offering is innovative or it's difficult for customers to under-stand how it can benefit them, consider offering a free trial so they can see it for themselves under no obligation, and ensure they receive something of value even if they don't proceed.

I try to share as much as I can, all in the spirit of abundance.

- I advocate others in my niche who I respect to my audience.
- I collaborate to make better products.
- I host a podcast to share stories of people's amazing business journeys.

- I post regular videos and share my knowledge and insight in my Facebook group.
- I offer a short quiz that provides a personalized report from my website.
- At certain times of the year, I also open my diary and offer a free one-to-one video call.

If you do things for free, be confident to ask for something small in return that will benefit you. It may be a review or a testimonial that will help grow your business, for example. It may be an introduction to someone in their network who could open new opportunities for you.

Action 4K

Consider what you can share for free that people will find valuable in the spirit of abundance.

- *How can this ultimately benefit your business?*

Ways of working

When your business gets going, you'll naturally embed processes, or ways of working. You'll have many tasks you'll need to complete, and they'll almost certainly need to be repeated at some stage.

I spoke with builder of sale-ready businesses Marianne Page to get her view on how you can optimize ways of working within your business, and Marianne answered three key questions.

- When is a good time to start systemizing a business?

Start early. For me, the earlier you start, the better. As a one-man band, finding the best way for you to complete a task, checking its logic and then recording it, you're making your own life easier when you come to repeat that task, but also building your training system for when you start to hire.

In McDonald's, there is only one right way to cook fries, and nobody would dream of doing it differently. There is one right way to do everything in the business, and that creates consistency and reliability. If every business had one right way of doing everything in its operation, it would have similar consistency and reliability.

Process is seen as bureaucratic, boring, dull – something that has to be done rather than something a business owner wants to do. The language can be scary, but for me a system is just a simple, logical, repeatable way of doing something.

Change the language around systems. Instead of talking about creating processes and standard operating procedures, talk about developing 'How To' guides. Using everyday language people are familiar with takes some of the fear away.

- With so many moving parts, where is the best place to start?

When I work with a business, I encourage it to start building one right way to do its most routine tasks – things it does every single day. Work out the best way to do all of those tasks. Then move on to tasks completed every week, every month, once per quarter, once a year.

- Which format do you suggest?

'How To' guides can be created as documents – step 1: do this, step 2: do this and so on – or as infographics or checklists, but the most effective format by far is video. If I want to learn something new I'll go to YouTube to find a video I can watch, rewind and pause until I really get to grips with the task I'm trying to learn. It's where most people go. So, I encourage business owners to create 'How To' videos for their tasks. It's such a simple way to systemize your business. Just record what you're doing.

The benefits of adopting this approach are huge. You'll create a slick business, you'll build assets, you'll deliver consistently for your customers and you'll begin to free yourself from the business, safe in the knowledge that it will continue to run how you want it to.

Removing the draining duplicated effort can free up time to focus on developing other areas of your business. It can make space in your mind to be creative when you've captured everything you need to.

When I first started writing this book I had the embryonic FUTURE Method recurring in my head for weeks. Once I wrote it down, it created space to develop it in more detail and also think about other approaches. The same may work for you with your business. The less energy you need to spend on repeatable tasks, the more creative you can be to grow.

Action 4L

Consider what repeatable tasks you complete, how often they occur and how you can create repeatable processes to make them consistent and simpler. Add the tasks to your plan and start recording your own 'How To' videos.

Growing your network

During Step 2: Understand, we looked at 'Getting to know the tribe' and deciding whether to make it your own. After you've committed to your business, a key step is to nurture and grow your personal network.

This will help you become known, liked and trusted and give you a platform to find and take opportunities.

It's a simple equation: the wider your network, the more opportunities will come your way and the more customers you'll gain.

As well as volume, consider the values, skill set and experience of those you bring into your network. The more branches you have, the wider your canopy and reach will be.

Keeping with the tree-related analogy, tech entrepreneur Paul Hulligan shares his thoughts on the benefits of growing a network.

> *As you're venturing into the unknown, it's invaluable to navigate the forest with people around you who know it well.*

If you're not confident at the prospect of networking, Paul's advice is simple.

> *If you want to succeed, learn to be good at it. The alternative is that people won't know who you are.*

During Step 3: Trial, we saw how Paul helped to found the 'Doc in a Day' competition at his social enterprise. Even as his main business has grown and he's scaled back other income-generating work, Paul has continued to run this, with a primary reason being the opportunity to grow his network and to inspire others. Paul explains.

It's like having a chip at the poker table. By chairing the competition, I'm seen as dynamic and a leader in my field. It gives me great visibility, and I get to grow my network every time we run it. Also, on a personal level, it's just very inspiring. There are so many stories of people who have come to the competition and it's helped change their career. It's about so much more than money.

Speaking at events or conferences is another reliable way of building your network and becoming more visible. They don't have to be big, especially initially, as you get more confident delivering your message and understanding what's possible.

In-person relationships are always stronger. It's how our brain is built. But the online options are vast.

Similar to speaking at events is running webinars. Even if it isn't an obvious option for your business, consider if there's an angle you can use to offer insight to your core customer. You may simply present, or you may offer a topic and open it up to a question and answer (Q&A) session led primarily by the audience and the problems they want to be resolved. You could also combine both approaches.

If a webinar isn't right for you – and it isn't for everyone – you can always record videos with handy tips showing examples of your work and publish them on social media platforms.

We've covered meetup.com, but there are also special-interest group features on many social media platforms that you can join or even start. I run a Facebook group called the *The Project Future Club*. This is a community for people like you taking steps to succeed as their own boss, which I created to enable people to share experiences, and ask questions.

The advice I've given for years is to accept connection requests on LinkedIn, as long as the profiles look genuine. They've approached you for a reason and may one day be a customer, supplier or partner.

Others also do this on Facebook, which is less formal and has the benefit of allowing a window into your life, showing that you're a real, relatable person rather than a professional who exists purely to power the economy. Somebody may quietly follow your journey then get in touch one day.

See the value in everyone you meet and how one day they may be useful to you. That may sound cold and impersonal, but many will take it as a compliment. If they aren't useful to you, they may be to someone else in your network and you can connect them for no personal gain. Both parties will appreciate the thought. Opportunities have come my way many times I've chosen to decline, and the next question is invariably 'is there anyone you can recommend?'

Whatever your method, keep the growth of your network in mind as part of your routine.

Action 4M

Develop a strategy to grow your network.

- *What platforms are right for you?*
- *What preparation will you need to complete in order to utilize the opportunities?*

Choose at least one approach to regularly engage in-person (where geography allows) and online. Evaluate your social media approach.

- *How could this become more useful to you as a base for your network?*

Finally, join my Facebook group today!

Making the most of your network

It's not all about new people. When I first launched my project management consultancy, I thought I was starting again and that I'd have to prove myself from the bottom to a new audience.

But that wasn't the case. Unexpectedly, and without pre-planning, my first contract came from a former manager who had also moved on since we previously worked together.

Being known, liked and trusted kick-started this new phase of my working life, with financial and other terms better than I initially requested. And that wasn't a one-off. I saw the benefit in this scenario quickly and realized it's much easier to sell something to someone you've sold to in the past. Since then, I've nurtured my network fondly as part of my routine and almost everywhere I've gone as a contractor has been with a friendly face nearby.

I may not have seen them in years, but just a quick 'hello', a response to a status update or even a 'Happy New Year' message is all it takes to get into someone's mind, plant the seed, and when they need someone you may have a willing client right in front of you. Away from strategy, it's also just a nice thing to do.

From a slightly different angle, review your personal network for skills and connections your friends and colleagues or former colleagues have. You might be pleasantly surprised.

Action 4N

- *How can you best utilize your network?*
- *Who can you reconnect with?*

Get advice from them and ask them for recommendations and introductions. Get their thoughts on how to maximize your plans.

Brand strategy

A brand is how you present your business. It's how you talk about it, and how you differentiate it from your competition. This results in how you're perceived publicly.

I spoke with brand transformation expert Vicki Young in detail about this. Vicki covered four key aspects.

- What are the benefits of branding, and what can a strong brand help you to achieve?

The right branding is the backbone that everything can hang off. It's how you talk to your team and your customers, how your website looks. It shapes new products so they're in line with the brand. It allows you to steer the business.

The brand identity part is really only the visual part. Often when people think about a brand they're thinking about a logo, colours, typeface and perhaps some photography or illustration. But it goes far deeper than that. It's about communicating the vision, mission and values of the business.

The reason branding is important to any business is to ensure it's positioning itself to be able to effortlessly talk to its customer so that, when it does, it's clear and relevant why the customer would choose it over its competitors.

Businesses have branding to set their story and their messaging, to set how they look and to ensure their marketing is consistent across all channels. I always describe it like this: you wouldn't turn up at an interview in fancy dress. That's exactly what could happen to your business if you don't consider how powerful a brand is.

- What makes a strong brand?

First you need to understand what your proposition is and your unique selling point (USP). What makes you different? How will you solve the problem differently? Then set the story. This all comes under the strategy work of a branding agency.

As part of the strategy work we do a piece around personas. Who are you trying to communicate to? Where are they? What are they interested in and why? Through your different audience personas, what are their pains, gains and needs?

All of that feeds into setting the story. What are the mission, vision and values of the business? How does that then translate into an elevator pitch?

Once you've got your story and set your fundamentals to say the right thing, it's then about reflecting them visually so you look the part too. People often make very quick decisions based on what something looks like before reading anything, so we need to make sure the visual element links in with what the business is about.

- How do you link a brand to a company name?

Many of our clients have established companies, and it's about rebranding and repositioning them in the market. We do also have people come to us with an unnamed product and a blank canvas.

When people come to us with a name already, it doesn't necessarily come preloaded with any emotional triggers. It's what you say and do around it that gives it that meaning. A name doesn't drive what the brand is about. So many names have been taken, so often people are coming up with names that aren't real words, like Zoopla, for example. That makes branding easier as you can apply your own meaning to it, which you can't do to descriptive names.

If you have something really descriptive which isn't aligned with the direction you want to go in, that can be a challenge.

- What pitfalls are to be avoided?

There are plenty of design No-Nos! Seriously, though, don't ever think your brand is fixed. It's a living, breathing, evolving thing that should adapt over time with your business. Your business might change and evolve, and you have to be willing to evolve with it. That's why plenty of businesses have rebrands. Looking at established brands, you can see how they've evolved and how they've listened to the market and adapted their positioning to respond.

We encourage businesses to look at the brand and see if there is a change in the market that means they need to flex their vision and mission. If you do this, ask yourself if there are any visual cues that need to be brought in to evolve them.

People often think they are designers. In the very early days, it's fine to do so and avoid spending money that could be better used elsewhere. However, you'll need to strike a balance to know when to switch and make your business look more credible, which is when branding and marketing become important; the two are aligned intrinsically and are absolutely crucial, but only at the right time. There is a fine art to it, and the most successful businesses know when to call in the professionals.

I found this interview fascinating, not just for Vicki's amazing insight into branding, but how the brand links up to so many other elements of the business. This interview was my second with Vicki, and took place after 95% of the book was written, but just how many of the sub-steps Vicki touched on still took me by surprise – 'Understanding your core customer', 'Values', 'Purpose, mission and vision statements' and 'Elevator pitch', to name but four. Your business is absolutely its own ecosystem, and in order to thrive every element needs to be integrated and harmonized.

Action 40

Create your brand strategy and develop your story.

- *How will you communicate your values, vision and mission via your brand?*
- *How will you reflect it visually?*
- *What part will your company name play in your brand?*
- *How will you assess the need to improve your brand?*
- *How will you choose the right time to invest in professional support?*

Communications strategy

Whereas a brand strategy is how you present your business, a communications strategy is the basis for how you reach your audience.

I spoke to communications expert Sara Price to get her take on it. Sara shared four tips for thinking clearly about communications strategy.

Tip 1: Recognize and accept that you need a communications strategy, and that having one will help you to reach your audience.

Think about your communications tactics as a trampoline. Your audience is on the other side of the garden fence and in order to be seen and heard by them, you use your trampoline to bounce up and down. Everybody loves jumping up and down on the trampoline, right?

And nearly everybody loves to go straight to tactics because that's the fun bit: coming up with a story idea, developing a new creative campaign for social media or brainstorming an event format. But your brilliant idea for Facebook is of no use if your clients are all on Instagram.

Your communications strategy is like the safety net around the trampoline. It stops you from bouncing off on a complete tangent and landing in the flower beds where nobody can see or hear you.

If you recognize that you need a strategy first, you'll be way ahead of most of your competitors who don't. You'll also avoid wasting time and effort doing things that won't deliver for you.

Tip 2: Understand that good communications exist to fulfil a purpose.

Good communications is not an end in itself. It's a means to an end. So, be clear on what your business objectives and priorities are and where communications can most help to support your business.

Tip 3: Work out which of the various communications tools at your disposal are best suited to the task.

External communications encompasses marketing, social media, public relations (PR), publicity, events and advertising. Each of these is a tool at your disposal.

In the same way you wouldn't use a spanner for every DIY task, you don't want to use the same communications tool for everything you're trying to achieve in your business. Sometimes advertising will be the most effective way to achieve your objectives. Sometimes it will be organic social media. Sometimes PR. Work out what's going to deliver for you and work with that – don't use a tool because you think you should or because everybody else does.

Tip 4: Don't just know your audience; truly understand them.

Every communications expert will tell you that 'know your audience/clients' is the first rule of good communications. I disagree.

First, I believe it's the first rule of business and it underpins every aspect of your business from the products you develop to the prices you charge.

Second, you don't just want to know your clients; you want to truly understand them. If you don't, then all of your communications are just guesswork.

You can then devise your communications as though you were speaking to just one person – your one ideal client. You want your clients and prospective clients to read your website or your social media posts and think: 'Wow, this person is talking to me!' You want them to feel seen and understood.

Just like my conversation with Vicki on brand strategy, Sara's insight here blew me away. The parallel in terms of brand identity and communications tactics being only a small part of the wider requirement is thought-provoking.

This also reinforces the point that each element works with others to form a business ecosystem, and getting it right is vital to your success.

In the following four sub-steps we look at where you'll present your business and how you can use communications tools to support your business.

Action 4P

Remind yourself of the core customer you identified in Step 2: Understand and ensure you deeply understand them in order to optimize your communications to them. Do your research and develop your communications strategy before thinking about creative tactics.

- *How will your communications strategy enable you to reach your audience?*
- *How can your business objectives be supported by communications?*
- *Which communications tools will you use for which tasks?*

Connecting with customers online

Even if your business is completely local and face-to-face, you'll be missing a trick if you don't have a presence online. There can be many different faces of an online presence. The hub or base station remains your company website, but there are also marketplace platforms that allow you to advertise your services and enable customers to find you based on their specific problem, and the big one – social media. Let's look at them one by one.

Website

Despite all the other ways people can learn about your business and get in touch with you online, having a strong website remains key.

A website is unique. It's your home, and it makes you credible. Once you own your website domain, which is quick and easy to buy from various internet domain registrars, it's yours to do with as you please.

You can create a sign-up page on your website where your audience can join your mailing list, or they can do this via something more value-adding for them, like an intelligent quiz. With a quiz, your potential customer will receive valuable, personalized information in exchange for sharing their email address. My quiz has received a fantastic response and is an example of getting around the 'what's in it for me?' question that your potential customer may ask themselves before submitting their email address. Always ensure the data you hold is compliant with local data protection regulations.

You can use your email list to communicate updates to your audience via a blog or a newsletter and share details of any product launches or events. In general, the engagement from those who have signed up to your mailing list is greater than that on social media, and the data is wholly yours – not dependent on somebody else's terms and conditions that could change at any time.

Interactions on other online platforms can be used to drive traffic to your website, where you can use it to showcase what your business stands for, provide examples of your work and drive an action from visitors to do something that you want them to do, with the end goal being for them to buy.

People's attention spans are short, and if your website is too noisy, unclear or all about you rather than about why it will benefit them, they will leave and may not come back.

A simple and professional thing to add is an email address using your domain. This looks so much more professional than using the name of an email service provider within your email address. These are little things that show potential customers you're in business, and you mean business.

Action 4Qi

Register your domain and add an email address. Get a skeletal version of your website published. Consider how to drive sign-up to your mailing list and how you'll structure your website to maximize sales.

Marketplaces

Depending on your type of business, you may be able to utilize online marketplaces. As we touched on when looking at the freelancer option and in 'Outsourcing' in Step 2: Understand, these work especially well for freelancers, but don't dismiss the option if your business is broader than that.

As an additional sales channel for you, it could broaden your reach and result in reduced marketing and advertising costs if you establish a presence and get positive reviews from customers.

It's often global, depending on the types of services you offer, meaning you could receive customers from anywhere, with payment managed by the platform.

Action 4Qii

Bespoke marketplaces are being launched regularly. Do an internet search for what you do followed by the word 'marketplace' to see your options.

Social media

Love it or hate it, one way or another social media will be key to growing and harnessing your network and building rapport with it going forward. Social media is just another form of networking, and sometimes you might have to work harder than for in-person networking. But once you've built your profile, it can make all the difference to how you're seen by your core customer, and also potential partners and collaborators.

I've had a strong LinkedIn presence since early in my professional life to maintain my network (feel free to add me – www.linkedin.com/in/robkerrauthor – stating that you've read this book), but I've never been strong on the other platforms. Therefore, I spoke with digital marketing expert Sophie Southmayd to get her insight and advice.

> *The number-one takeaway is you need to be authentic. We are living in a world with fake news and where everyone is trying to sell something, using filters, modifying pictures and that kind of thing. Gone are the days of that 'perfect lifestyle' and people are really pushing against that. In the beauty industry, for example, the brands that are performing the best are the ones that are poking fun at those pursuing the stereotypical barbie-girl image.*

As we've looked at in 'Brand strategy' and 'Communications strategy' above, consistency is key in terms of message and delivery. You can choose any tone of delivery for your message, regardless of your industry, as long as you're consistent. If you start cheeky, your followers will like it and be alarmed if you suddenly go formal. The reverse is also true.

Consistency is also vital for the algorithms that choose whether to display your post or someone else's. Sophie continues.

> *All the platforms want to see that you're on there regularly, and they can rely on you to be on there, and then they will push your content.*

> *It's about genuine community management, interacting with your clients. If they're writing to you, you should write back and build rapport – people appreciate that and they're more likely to want to work with you as a result.*

I asked Sophie about what approach makes an impact.

People don't follow brands. People follow humour, figures and advice. We need to spice it up a bit; for example, make the posts about female empowerment. It may be that it's a jewellery brand but that doesn't matter – it's a female-empowered jewellery brand. It's about recognizing who your audience is and what speaks to them.

Home cooking educator Dani Mosley started sharing meal plans that she was making for her family on her personal Instagram account well before starting her business, but it proved the catalyst to show that she had something people were interested in and has continued to be a core part of her communications. Dani explains.

People want inspiration and that's what the meal plans offer.

There are so many social media platforms out there. In the early days at least, you're unlikely to be able to make a big impression on all of them, so consider where your customers are, then focus your energy on maintaining those. Sophie shares more on this.

Whatever platforms you choose, be aware that video is the present and future of social media. I encourage all of my clients to publish video content. It can be intimidating to shoot content of yourself, but it's worth getting over the fear. Our attention span is so short now that videos wake up our brain.

It isn't an instant process and it may take a long time for a customer to feel ready to approach you. I know from my own experience; I've followed people's output for years before I've contacted them and signed up to some of their premium services seemingly out of the blue. But it wasn't out of the blue; I just hadn't felt the need to make myself known until the time was right.

What I have found with social media is that the conversion rate is often very low. When I put up a video on LinkedIn introducing my plans for this book and asking for people to get in touch if they wanted to share their stories, over 3,000 people saw it. Of those, 59 liked it, three added comments and three shared it. What mattered most was that seven got in touch and they became contributors to the book. They also introduced me to others who became contributors that were previously outside of my network. With the wide reach social media offers, if you're strategic, the right people will see your communications and follow up with you.

When it comes to waiting for things to be perfect in terms of the quality of your posts, Sophie ends with another top tip.

> *Just get it out there. Don't worry about it being perfect; it never will be, and it's probably way better than you think.*

Action 4Qiii

Work out which one or two social media platforms will serve you best and how you can engage with your core customer beyond your brand. Even if you're not actively working on your business yet, start growing your social media profile now. It will benefit you to have that history and network when you're ready. Think about how often you'll post and how it aligns to your communications strategy.

- *How will it benefit your audience?*
- *What hook will you use to make them feel part of your community?*

Marketing campaigns and advertising

As part of your communications to your network, consider developing specific marketing campaigns. Campaigns are goal-driven, targeted and only run for a predefined period of time.

For example, you may be running a training programme and want 20 people to sign up. In the weeks (or even months) ahead of this, you may attend, exhibit or speak at events where your core customers gather. You may publish content in relation to it online. You may advertise. Or you may run smaller, cheaper events on the basis that, having come to know, like and trust you, a percentage of the attendees will register for the higher-value programme.

When running a campaign, you'll normally increase your volume of communications. This may include increased spend on advertising.

Covering advertising more generally, your biggest return is likely to be online, due to the algorithms used to make sure the adverts are targeted to your audience. From 'Understanding your core customer' in Step 2: Understand and 'Communications strategy' above, you'll be able to determine a starting point for this.

I asked digital marketing expert Sophie Southmayd for her best tips about advertising on social media.

> *Put aside £30–40 per week for sponsored posts. It may be £10 on X post, £15 on Y post, but the key takeaway to make sure you're not wasting your money is to understand your analytics and to understand impressions, reach and engagement. For example, if a lot of traffic comes in between 6pm and 8pm on Wednesdays, let's post things or launch products in that time slot, when the audience is active. It's about learning to read between the lines.*

Action 4R

Think through how you could implement two to four marketing campaigns each year within your business.

- *When would they be?*
- *What would your goals be?*
- *Who would you target?*
- *How would you measure success?*
- *How will you utilize advertising, both generally and within your campaigns?*

Events

Exhibiting at events is an option to grow your profile and make people more aware of you. In an increasingly digital world, physically being present and talking to potential customers about your offering can make you stand out.

Even if your business doesn't have products to sell on the day, people can place orders, or you can hand out discount codes if they purchase after the event.

Some events are purely industry-focused and national or even international in their reach. But equally, they can be focused on an event in itself, such as a wedding, where businesses from various industries that enable the wedding to happen will exhibit. This includes venues, jewellers, florists, photographers, DJs, stylists, wedding cars – you get the picture.

An event like a wedding fair takes place in most towns and cities in the UK, and I dare say elsewhere. Early on, these smaller events will most likely be more suitable for you to exhibit at.

Fine jewellery aficionado Trang Do explains her approach.

> *My business is mainly online, so I exhibit at events to be as physically present as possible. People like to know you exist, and this is part of how I get in front of my audience.*
>
> *I exhibit at events all year round, but specifically focus on events aligned to my key marketing campaigns ahead of the summer wedding season, and in the build-up to Christmas.*

Even if you're not ready to exhibit, take a look at what is out there. Attending some events will give you clarity on the approach of others, both in your market and beyond. You can often take inspiration from other industries and put a unique twist on your own approach. This will also provide experience of what the event is like and you'll find out if it's right for you when it comes around again.

In addition to formal events, there are networking events and workshops that you can attend and often offer to present at. You may not be paid (initially, at least) but that isn't the point.

If you see an opportunity, you may also plan your own events, alone or with complementary businesses.

Action 4S

Find out what key industry events take place, where they are and when. Look at multi-industry events that your customers attend, and unique events that may work for you. Contact the event management to get an idea of the cost for a stand and dates you'd need to commit by. Get a view on the number of attendees, and how their profile aligns to that of your core customer. This will enable you to estimate the number of leads, the quality of those leads and therefore the likely return on your investment. Look for networking events and workshops, start attending then offer to be a speaker.

Public relations and publicity

Public relations (PR) and publicity can enable you to reach more of your core customers and build your profile. It will also provide material that you can use afterwards to promote and differentiate yourself from your competition.

PR is controlled internally within your business. You decide which material to release, whereas publicity is externally controlled by those choosing to write or talk about you. Therefore, we'll focus on PR.

There are various types of PR, but for your scenario, the most relevant is media relations. PR differs from advertising as you don't need to pay for it, but in order to be successful at PR you'll have to earn it, by convincing the right person to feature you. Earning the right to be featured gives an external, or third-party, validation that even expensive advertising campaigns cannot achieve.

Let's specifically look at appealing to journalists. You'll need to turn your messages into stories that will appeal to journalists and their audience, and build mutually beneficial relationships with them.

Bear in mind, journalists don't just reach their audience via the traditional print and broadcast mediums; there is also digital journalism in the form of online magazines, special-interest groups, blogs, social media and more.

Find journalists who may be able to convey and share your story and follow them for a while before contacting them asking for something. If they don't know who you are, or anything about your business, why would they be interested? If you interact with a journalist and are useful to them without asking for anything in return, for example, by answering questions they pose, then when you do ask they're more likely to accommodate you.

If you have a sizable profile online, there is always the chance that you'll be approached, but if you want to get ahead and be visible in multiple places I certainly don't suggest sitting back and waiting for the phone to ring.

Home cooking educator Dani Mosley shares her experience.

> *My PR came in different forms. I approached a local newspaper, the Dulwich Diverter, and asked if they would like me to write a recipe for them. They said yes! I did the same with the Co-op Food magazine. They also said yes.*
>
> *Then with BBC Good Food, I had self-published one of my recipes on their website, which anyone can do, and they approached me and asked if they could publish it in the magazine. I was delighted! The Daily Telegraph approached me. I have also approached a few other food magazines and they never even replied to my emails, so it was quite hit-and-miss, but I figured I had nothing to lose each time.*

I think that's such a strong point – apart from the knock to your ego from rejection and the time spent crafting your pitch to them, you have nothing to lose in this scenario. If you keep getting rejected or ignored, you'll know to modify your approach.

Be clear on the reasons behind choosing PR as a communications tool before you commit to it, though. Communications expert Sara Price explains.

> *People come to me and say they need to do PR. My first question is 'why?'. What often becomes clear very quickly is they've not really thought about what their business is trying to achieve, or whether PR is the right way to support that. I spend as much time telling people they're not ready for PR as I do actually advising them on PR. Don't look to be in the media for the sake of it.*

Action 4T

Decide if PR is the right communications tool to help you achieve your business goals. Look at articles that will appeal to a similar audience to yours and see how they are structured,

> *and how the business owner shapes their story. Make a list of journalists, both local and national, who may be interested in your story and start to build a relationship with them.*

Getting your image right

When you're in business, you'll be judged regularly. Some of these judgements will matter, and some won't. Some you can do something about, and others will be completely outside of your control.

Getting your image right will be key to how you're perceived in those first-impressions scenarios before people decide to do business with you.

When my dad, David Kerr, started his own business, his offering was laying and fixing industrial floors. He'd often go to big warehouse units, meet the client, measure up and quote. He was always conscious to appear professional and reputable, but not flash. On one occasion, though, he slipped up. He explains.

Normally, my arrival in a big customer car park was barely noticed. One day, visiting a potential new client, I took my BMW 7 Series. When I met the client in the car park, instead of saying 'hello', he simply stated, 'you'll be expensive'.

As I measured and priced the job, I knew I was wasting my time. I may have given the most reasonable quote possible and delivered a brilliant service, but the perception the client had from that first impression cost me any chance of the contract.

I asked him what he changed as a result.

I never took the BMW to site again! From then on, I took a Nissan Navara pick-up truck. This was a functional vehicle; it had space for materials to be dropped at site, and four seats for staff, should either be needed. But it very much wasn't a van nor a high-performance car. It struck the right balance for first impressions with a client that this person could be trusted to do the job, yet not charge over the odds.

Action 4U

Think about interactions you've had in the past.

- *Where has the first impression made a big positive or negative impact for you?*
- *How can you make your image consistent to your brand and please as many customers as possible, whilst staying true to your personality and business needs?*

Your offering and pricing

I've placed consideration of your offering and pricing at the end of the visible sub-steps, as I think having clarity on all of the strategic and visible sub-steps will enable you to create a better offering to delight your core customer.

Work out how you can create a range of products and services that require different levels of commitment. This range will enable you to initially convert more leads into sales, and then as you build the relationship with your customer you'll be in a position to achieve higher-priced or repeat sales.

This range of products and services will enable you to generate the margins that will make your business a success.

In the 'Abundance' sub-step above, I explained how I share as much as I can for free. As well as being how I choose to live my life, this forms part of my offering and has the benefit of generating leads – meaning attracting and engaging with potential customers. My free material allows someone to consider whether what I offer will be of value to them. If it isn't, I've lost nothing.

On the other hand, if they decide I can add value, they may go on to purchase one of my lower-priced products to effectively trial me before committing to a higher-priced part of my offering where I work with them to achieve their business goals, satisfaction and balance.

There is no need to hide from this strategy. I want to attract and engage people, and both my free and lower-priced products offer significant standalone value. If someone then signs up to my core value-adding offering I want them to be 100% aware of what they are signing up to, and the benefit they can expect to receive.

Position your offering on the result it will give your customers, rather than simply what it is. As covered in 'Understanding your core customer' in Step 2: Understand, being clear you can resolve their problem (in the form of a need or want) will make you stand out.

For example, if you're a jeweller, you don't simply provide a wedding ring. You're part of the experience and provide a visual reminder of the happiest day of your customer's life. It's a slightly different angle, but will communicate to your customers why they need you.

When presenting your offering, make the journey clear to your potential customers. If they buy, what will they have to do, and what will you do in return?

To follow up on the approach we covered in 'Ways of working' above, coding and naming your products or services will provide a consistent approach when selling and makes tracking metrics simpler. For example, if your product has a code you can use this shorthand name within internal processes, including loading it into a point-of-sale payment tool that will enable you to take card payments. A good name, on the other hand, will make the product relatable and aspirational to your audience.

Finally, think carefully about your pricing. Your free and lower-priced offering notwithstanding, your higher-priced offering needs to have a high mark-up, and you need to be able to sell enough of them, otherwise you won't have a business. Customers are not offended by you making a profit, but they must accept the balance between the prices you charge and the value they'll receive from you resolving their problem.

Steer clear from linking your time with money when you consider pricing your offering. It's not about time; it's about the benefit your customers will receive.

Action 4V

- *What range of products and services will you create to form your offering?*
- *How will you attract and engage your customers?*

> - *How, and what, will you sell?*
> - *How will you structure your pricing?*

Working environment

The chances are, if you've been in regular employment for some time, you've been used to a regular desk, a commute to get there and perhaps some time working from home. As your own boss, this is likely to change.

Even in the most comparable self-employment scenario, contracting, 'the office' becomes 'client site' and 'working from home' becomes 'working from X office', with 'X' being the name of your company.

DevSecOps consultant Glenn Wilson puts it like this.

> *When I'm not on client site, I am very clear to state I am working from my company's office, even though that happens to be at home. I see it with other consultants I work with from larger companies when they aren't on-site; they are at their company office, and it's exactly the same for me.*
>
> *Although it's only a small mindset shift, the room I have set aside is more than a home office; it's my company headquarters and treating it like that is valuable for me and the perception of the client that I'm in a working environment.*

Set up your home office the best you can to make it a comfortable working environment. Ideally, this would be a separate room. Ours doubles as the guest bedroom, but with a sofa bed it feels like an office when it's used as such. Invest in a quality chair and ensure the space works for you. After all, you'll be spending a lot of time there.

In addition to perception, it may be that working from home doesn't work for you mentally, as it can be difficult to make the distinction between home life and work life, and as such the temptation is to never switch off and effectively be at work all the time.

In the early days of her company, brand transformation expert Vicki Young used to make a conscious effort to go for a walk in the morning, even if she had nowhere to go, to effectively replicate the mentality of the commute and therefore 'arrive' ready for work.

Especially early on when you're developing your business and may not have many customers, if you're working from a laptop the reality is you can work from anywhere. Investing in your own office is an option but may be an expense you don't need initially.

There is the option to hire a space in a coworking office, or even ask for space in an existing office – especially if they may be a good partner in future. Glenn explains.

> Leasing an area at the office of a local business provides a space for formal client meetings, as well as a place to work without too many distractions. It may even lead to opportunities to gain new business if your landlord shares a common customer base.

Working from your home office is of course an option if you have space, and comes at little cost, as does working from a coffee shop or library. My personal preference is to work from the café in my local gym.

There are also societies or members' clubs you can join that have other benefits such as a like-minded community in addition to working space, for example, Soho House, and may not be as expensive as you think when compared to paying for a standard desk space somewhere. However, such clubs can have a long waiting list and selective membership criteria.

In other scenarios, you may need to travel due to the needs of your customers or get into a routine with cyclical conferences, exhibitions, local business meetups and sales campaigns that become vital to your business.

Your customers may be in various locations where you have to be mobile or it may be necessary for you to have a physical base.

Action 4W

Ensure your working environment suits you and your customers.

- *How will it need to flex to fulfil the various requirements your business demands from you?*
- *How can you optimize comfort, cost and convenience and make sure it's conducive to the needs of your customers?*

Discipline within the working day

If you've been used to a rigid routine for some time, it could prove a culture shock to have nobody to answer to apart from yourself, and easy to give in to distractions.

Building on what we covered in the 'Working environment' sub-step above, creating your own routines and disciplines will be key to your productivity and sense of achievement.

People often describe themselves as a 'self-starter' on their CV, but as your own boss this is vital to your success. It's the tenacity we covered within the SORTED Framework.

Having a work ethic to get things done and avoid distractions or simply waste time procrastinating is what often makes the difference between those who succeed and those who don't. Some do it naturally, whereas others need to draw strict boundaries. I'm more towards the latter side, and have built a routine that works for me.

As your own boss, you're effectively doing two jobs. You're working for your customers, but also running your own business – managing business development and the pipeline of new work, managing invoices, expenses and admin by working with at least an accountant, if not other suppliers and partners.

In my early days as my own boss, client work took absolute priority, just like when I was in employment. It took about two years for me to think running the business wasn't a chore and to stop putting the paperwork off until the deadline. And that was in a simple business! Anything more complex, with multiple customers, suppliers, products or services, or even having staff, will require more extensive oversight and control.

Regardless of the complexity and structure of your business, I recommend planning your day/week/month via a calendar. In addition to my computer calendar, I find blocking time in the family calendar on the fridge not only secures it as 'working time', but also makes me accountable to them and myself that I'm using the time productively.

Action 4X

Assess how driven and self-motivated you are naturally and the level of intervention that will benefit you.

- *What routines and disciplines will work for you?*
- *How will you make the most of your time?*
- *How will you prioritize and fulfil the complex needs of your business?*

Making time away from work

Having discipline to the working day isn't just about work. It also serves to protect your non-working time, including your social life, via your leisure time, those essential things you need to do and your downtime to achieve the lifestyle aspirations we covered in Phase 1.

Having boundaries and a clear distinction between work and play removes that feeling of guilt when you're not working, and the temptation to work all the time. To do this, I make a point on the calendar to clearly define downtime and capture social or family events that are important to me at the start of each planning cycle.

A planning cycle is normally quarterly for me, but it can be annually if you know about bigger events like holidays far enough in advance. I also look to refine it monthly when more detailed, smaller events are known such as the children's school plays.

Thinking back to the architect's example I shared in 'Lifestyle' in Step 2: Understand, they chose not to work during school holidays and planned their business around those dates. It was 'non-negotiable' for them. If I disagreed, they were happy to politely decline my business. Although a relatively extreme example, you can successfully run a business around non-negotiables like that if you prioritize them and communicate them clearly.

It comes back to the mindset of valuing your time and your personal priorities, but then also finding solutions to work around them.

Within the working day itself, unless you're committed to client work as a contractor, some working days can be shorter than others and only you can make the decision as to what is right. You may decide to finish at lunchtime on a Friday, for example, and build this into your routine.

Action 4Y

Decide on the regularity of your planning cycles and allocate time for them as part of your plan. Block the time out in your calendar when you don't intend to work at the start of each planning cycle.

- *What are your non-negotiables?*
- *How will you plan your work around them and communicate them?*

Rewarding yourself

In addition to planning time away from work, you should absolutely plan to reward yourself in whatever way works best for you. It's another mindset shift, as I know it doesn't always come naturally or feel important. With no boss, though, nobody else is going to say thanks apart from yourself and there are significant personal and professional benefits to justify it.

I spoke with leadership and life coach Sue Belton about this. Sue explains.

> *A reward gives a dopamine hit, which makes you happy. I work with super-high achievers who are massively driven but often have low self-worth. Their whole self-worth is linked to achievement, so they never feel as though they've done enough to deserve a reward. This is often linked to imposter syndrome.*
>
> *I help them hold on to the positives but remove the view that nothing is ever good enough, as this means they cannot enjoy their achievements. It's often the pushy-parent mentality of 'what next?'. The first step is identifying that voice which gives the limiting belief that has you feeling you're not good enough*

*unless you constantly achieve. The second step is to be aware of
the voice and modify behaviour next time it happens.*

I build targets and little rewards into my working day. For example,
during the writing process for this book, whilst in the gym café, I
committed to writing 1,000 words each morning before I considered
going for a run or a swim. I then knew I had more time in the afternoon to get as much done as I could before doing the school run. As
I'm generally less creative in the evening, I tended to complete any
admin tasks after the kids had gone to bed before settling down to
relax (a reward in itself).

There are also longer-term rewards that you can plan after reaching
a key milestone or achieving an objective. Sticking with my book-
writing example, I scheduled a weekend break after the first draft was
due for submission to my publisher. I find a natural break like this
invaluable. Knowing a significant milestone has been reached means
the reward can be enjoyed without guilt and provides the opportunity
to reset and prepare for your next objective.

Action 4Z

Consider if anything is preventing you rewarding yourself.

- *What simple targets and rewards can you build into your
  day?*
- *What bigger rewards can you give yourself after a significant achievement?*

Retrospective

As you get to the end of Step 4: Undertake, you should have clarity on
your options to create a plan that will support the delivery of your key
objectives during the early life of your business.

There's a lot to digest here and you may need to come back to different
sub-steps as you do further research to develop then implement your
plan.

A key takeaway is how so many elements of your business link together
to form its own ecosystem.

Let's briefly look over what was covered.

Initially, we looked at the *strategic* sub-steps. They are the goals and objectives of what your business plans to achieve, and how you'll achieve it.

We then looked at the *visible* sub-steps. This is how your business will look and feel.

Finally, we looked at the *personal* sub-steps. This is how the business should facilitate your lifestyle and those included in your impact factor.

There is no gate or Steering Meeting at the end of Step 4: Undertake as its key milestone is to baseline your Phase 2 plan, covered at the start. The next key sign-off comes after its parallel, Step 5: Review.

Let's go there now.

Step 5: Review

The scope

Whether formal or informal, everything you do in your business should be considered and evaluated. If your reviews stay close to what you're undertaking, and you and your stakeholders are open and honest, you should steer your business on the right path.

In this step you'll discover a range of tools, techniques and considerations to enable you to review successfully.

At the end of the step, we consider when you might need the advice of your SteerCo beyond your regular meeting rhythm.

Let's start reviewing!

The review

A review is used in project management to take a breather and check on progress.

There are lots of review metrics and different audiences for these reviews. Some are scheduled as regular checkpoints, some are linked to delivering an objective and some are required due to unexpected events – either as a result of something that has happened internally or from the external environment.

Reviews are also held with suppliers and customers as a way of checking in on progress and improving relationships.

Scheduling regular reviews into your business, and making necessary decisions as an outcome, should result in clarity, no surprises for you or your stakeholders and solid alignment with your business goals (or indeed, the opportunity to agree on changes to them in a timely manner).

Building on the low-risk failure strategy we covered in Step 3: Trial, the review will add value if you overstretch or commit to something that you don't want to be doing. It will enable you to get back on track quickly, and reduce the pain.

Although the review runs parallel to the work you'll undertake to build your business, many of the review processes you put in place during the early life of your business will continue when you move into Step 6: Expand, although during a more settled period they may become more light-touch.

Action 5A

Think back to reviews you've had previously in your working life.

- *What positives can you take from them as you build your own reviews?*

Consider what you want to achieve from your reviews, and how they can enable you to set objectives to achieve your business goals.

The INPUTS Review Framework

Just as in Phase 1 when signing off your INPUTS business case, to keep things in balance your business must continue to work for you and your family.

Therefore, when looking at the scope of a review, let's reconsider how the INPUTS factors can be applied within a review, via the INPUTS Review Framework.

- The **I**mpact review: recognition of what impact your business is having on key people in your life. Has this been in line with what you agreed?
- The **N**umbers review: an examination of business finances. How do your costs and revenue compare to your plan? Consider forecast, actuals and any variance. Is the business generating sufficient net profit for your personal needs?
- The **P**ersonal review: to determine whether the business is making you happy and is still aligned with your values. Have you been able to take the time you planned away from work and have you looked after yourself?
- The **U**seful review: consideration of what skills you have sourced externally. How successful have they been? Has your way of working been adopted successfully? What is the next priority to support your team or customers?
- The **T**iming review: an appraisal of your plan. Are you on target to achieve the objectives and goals you've set? How accurate has your requirements sizing been? How strong was your baseline plan and how many new requirements or changes have you brought in?
- The **S**ales review: have you met your sales targets? Which parts of your offering have over- or under-performed? What opportunities and threats lie ahead? How can you delight your customers further?

For each consideration of your reviews, add a RAG status to capture the overall position. A simple definition is below.

- **R**ed: falls below expectation and needs addressing now.
- **A**mber: at risk of not meeting expectation; to watch or make minor adjustments.
- **G**reen: on track and no current concerns.

In addition to these three, I include a blue status to mark things that are done.

Not all considerations will be covered in each review, but having this template as your starting point will help you to determine the right scope for the right forum.

Action 5B

Develop a template based on the INPUTS Review Frame-work with your priorities in each of the six areas. Use this as a starting point when deciding the scope of each of your reviews.

Types of review

There are broadly two types of review within a project – the gate review, and the checkpoint review.

Gate reviews take place at the end of a project phase or upon the completion of a strategic objective. The sign-off of your business case at the end of Phase 1 is an example of a gate review.

Going forward, other examples of a gate review could be the launch of a product, a marketing campaign or running an event. You'll want to review the outcomes and lessons learned. If it hasn't met your expectations, what impact does that have on your plans going forward? Do you need to modify or cancel the next step as a result, or even a long-term goal? Equally, if it has gone well, what opportunities does this create and how can you maximize them?

Checkpoint reviews, on the other hand, are defined by time. They are scheduled to repeat weekly, fortnightly or monthly. These are used to assess progress and may run at different levels in your business. You may decide to hold regular one-to-one meetings with members of your team, host a team meeting or keep a regular Steering Meeting in your rhythm, or cadence, as a decision-making forum.

When to review, and how many reviews you have, will depend on the needs of your business.

Some reviews will be requested by, or for the benefit of, your suppliers or customers. This is a natural part of the cycle and will ensure the relationships remain strong. If they aren't requesting the review, consider raising the topic with them.

If external stakeholders or members of your team are required to be present or contribute material to the review, ensure you give them enough time to prepare and a submission deadline, and that you're clear on what is expected of them at the meeting.

Action 5C

Plan your meeting cadence. Consider the following.

- *What reviews will you hold?*
- *How frequent will they be?*
- *What will trigger a gate review?*
- *What checkpoint reviews will you hold?*
- *How will you engage your SteerCo going forward?*
- *In what circumstances would you hold a review with an external stakeholder like a supplier or customer?*
- *How will you ensure the material prepared by others is available in time?*

Reviewing with a mentor or buddy

As your business evolves and gets its own identity, working with a mentor regularly could add significant value by clarifying your thinking, and keeping you accountable to yourself.

A mentor will work with you to set realistic goals and possibly be bolder than your natural instinct would allow. Perhaps what they suggest is too bold, but it's always worth the conversation and you can assess where the right balance should be.

Equally, if you've gone off on a tangent and are being unrealistic in your plans or not true to the foundations your business was built on, they'll be able to see it and, if they're a good mentor, won't hold back in telling you about it.

We first touched on a mentor when considering who to invite onto your SteerCo, so if you get one, make sure you ask them.

A mentor tends to be someone in your field with more knowledge or experience than you. In addition to them, or even instead of them, it can also be useful to hold regular meetings with a buddy.

I see the relationship with a buddy, in our context rather than its definition in a corporate setting, as an equal partnership. A suitable buddy will run a different type of business to you and have their own goals and challenges. If you're each more experienced in some areas that are relevant to you both and provide advice and support to each other it can maintain the healthy equality of this partnership.

I meet with my buddy weekly on a Monday. We talk through how we got on with our targets from the previous week, our plans for the coming week and any concerns with achieving longer-term goals.

This really helps me with accountability, both to get things finished and also to have a clear plan for the week ahead. It also averts some of the loneliness that comes from not working in a physical team environment.

Be it a mentor or a buddy, having someone involved who is external to the day-to-day running of your business means they'll see things from a different angle and may spot opportunities or offer solutions that you haven't considered.

It can be scary to open up to somebody outside of your business, especially if it's someone you look up to, but as we know there is a lot of value in feeling uncomfortable.

Action 5D

If you haven't got a mentor or a buddy, look into getting one from your network or start building a relationship with someone who you think will do a great job. Consider if you need both and the frequency of each. For example, you may meet with a buddy more regularly than a mentor.

Change control

Change control is used to make sure you, and those to whom it matters in your business, are aware of what is changing in terms of your plan, your objectives or goals. It allows you to retain control and is an acknowledgement that you're in agreement with the approach going forward.

When you sign off your plan for each phase, it becomes baselined. You have clear tasks to complete and targets to meet. If you're reviewing this and something in the plan has changed – be it the timing, the cost or the scope – or something new has appeared that you'd like to divert time, money or effort to as a higher priority than something already on your plan, then it should be reviewed and assessed.

Your stakeholders should be clear on their roles ahead of any review, such as whether they are consulted ahead of the decision or simply informed of the outcome.

A simple change control form covering the six considerations of the INPUTS Review Framework can be completed for this purpose, covering what is changing and why. If a factor isn't impacted, it can be flagged as n/a.

A formal decision is then made, and the outcome is communicated to all impacted stakeholders.

Once the change has been approved, this is your new baseline. Plans, forecasts and RAID logs should be updated accordingly to factor in the change, and the impact it has had on other objectives or goals.

Action 5E

Consider how and when you should implement change control.

- *How will you ensure stakeholder alignment, acceptance and communication of the changes?*

Forecast, actuals and variance

In a corporate setting, forecast, actuals and variance data fall into the realm of accountants – normally within a month-end process.

For you, however, it's unlikely to be something your accountant will want to be involved with (they tend to look at the actuals only). Let's look at each in turn and consider how they apply to you.

A *forecast* is what you expect to happen within a set period of time. It's normally over a monthly period, but you can choose to forecast in line with your checkpoint meetings as you feel appropriate.

I suggest you have a detailed forecast maintained for the next six months, and then look further ahead at a high level, in line with your long-term goals from your three-year plan. Thinking ahead strategically will enable you to create the detailed near-term forecast you'll need to hit in order to achieve your bigger business goals.

You can add a weighting to your forecast in the format of a likelihood percentage to support planning. The further ahead you're looking, the lower your confidence will be due to what can change in this period. For example, signed contracts can be 99% or even 100% likely for next month, but maybe only 80% in three months' time if there is a notice period in the contract. Pipeline work that is likely but not confirmed could be 70% likely next month but 50% in three months' time.

Accountants I once worked with used the concept of 'unidentified future opportunities' (UFO for short). Your likelihood percentage for UFO may be low, perhaps 30% or less, but once you get into a rhythm with your business it's something you can consider to forecast more accurately.

Actuals are what has actually happened. Corporate accountants normally collate the actuals as part of their month-end process. I strongly suggest you do too.

Variance is the difference between the forecast and the actuals. This is normally the key output of the corporate accountant's month-end process, where management assess whether targets were met and what follow-up action is needed, including revising future forecasts and business goals.

It may be that you choose to capture and review forecasts and actuals, and therefore the variance between the two, for some or all of your INPUTS review factors – but certainly for your numbers and more strategically with sales.

The real effort here is in the forecast. If your forecast is good, by the time you get actuals your variance should be small. Even if your actuals are well above your forecast, this could be seen as a negative as you won't have been able to plan properly to support your business.

Either way, a big variance means you're likely to have had to be reactive rather than proactive when managing your business. A strong forecast will aid control and generally make for a better experience for all stakeholders.

In addition to control, a well-considered forecast will also support capacity planning, which we look at next.

Action 5F

Consider which of your INPUTS metrics you want to forecast and track. There is a case for all six, but some will be a greater priority to you than others.

- *How will you capture the actuals and when will you review the variance?*
- *How will you weight your forecast for confirmed and planned work?*
- *How far ahead will you forecast and how often will you update plans as a result?*

Capacity planning

Unlike in a job of employment, your role and responsibilities as a business owner are not defined or limited. As your business grows, so does the amount of stuff that needs to be done, and the boring, easy, repeatable stuff doesn't go away. You may be finding yourself stretched, spending too much time working, and your business has reached capacity in its current form.

Your forecast is the basis for the capacity you need to plan for in order to continue to meet the needs of your business. It can take time to get team members or suppliers on board – or release them – to ensure you're prepared for the needs of your business.

Cash-flow is king, as we've seen, and it absolutely works alongside your capacity to accept a contract to ensure you don't over-trade.

During your checkpoint reviews, consider what, when and how you can outsource, collaborate with others or grow your team (we cover the latter two in Step 6: Expand). This is to take the pressure off yourself, but also to enable your business to grow with the right balance of partners.

If your capacity is higher than you need, review the notice periods you have for supplier contracts or premises to ensure you're not paying for things you don't require.

If you find yourself forecast to be under-utilized, remember that you're never 'unemployed' and consider what tasks and objectives you can personally deliver to grow your business.

Action 5G

Consider your current capacity, and how you can use your forecast to ensure your business is prepared for the challenges ahead.

- *How quickly can you vary your capacity in response to an opportunity or threat?*

Emergency changes

Sometimes things won't go to plan and there's nothing you can do about it. In many respects, that's life. Something unexpected may happen and you have to drop everything as a result and focus on fixing this one thing the best you can.

When I worked in technology, this kind of scenario would happen more often than the boss would like, and the mechanism in place to resolve it was called an emergency change.

During a major incident – for example, when the website was down or something had failed, affecting customers' ability to go about their days – normal processes and rules for making the changes essentially go out of the window. A dedicated team comes together to resolve it as quickly as possible and the boss is often briefed, with special approval given to make changes to the system outside of the normal change windows.

This can often be a chaotic time in the technology department, but almost always the scenario has been considered and there's a process in place to resolve the issue.

I hope you don't have to go through anything quite so urgent. However, unexpected things will happen to your business where you'll need to take swift action.

Looking back at brand transformation expert Vicki Young's example of losing a major client early in the life of her business, it can mean priorities have to be reset and your focus may need to change.

When an unexpected scenario does impact you and your plans, try not to panic but instead take a step back and assess the size of the issue, what is affected, what you can do to resolve it and when.

Once remedial action has taken place, schedule regular reviews (with your SteerCo or wider stakeholders as necessary) to assess how successful the resolution was and what further effort may be required to avoid a repeat.

I always try to stay optimistic, and it may be that an emergency change is required for positive reasons where a new opportunity has appeared that may completely alter the dynamic of your business, potentially for the better.

Be it negative or positive, focusing the right level of your resources and those of your team on resolving an issue that requires emergency intervention and getting back to business-as-usual as quickly as possible will be a key challenge to overcome.

Action 5H

Put in place a process for managing emergency changes, including escalations to decision-makers at relevant suppliers. Consider what scenarios could occur and add them as risks to your RAID log. Put in place a regular review meeting to ensure your RAID log is accurate and comprehensive.

Lessons learned

During any project, it's important to keep an eye on lessons learned. When something new happens that could potentially happen again, you simply note down the scenario and what you did about it. You can also look more generally.

This is reflection time, when you take a step back and consider what went well and what didn't go quite so well. You can then actively consider this when the scenario reoccurs or during your next planning cycle.

From my experience, lessons learned are normally considered at the end of the project, which I feel is a wasted opportunity. If you keep them in mind during each of your checkpoint reviews and capture them accordingly, the information will be fresh, and you'll be more likely to make use of it next time it becomes relevant. By doing so, you'll continuously improve your ways of working and your efficiency, and your business should improve.

Some lessons learned may naturally stand out, but for inspiration use the six factors within the INPUTS Review Framework as a starting point.

Action 51

Start a lessons learned log and build this into your checkpoint reviews as an agenda item. Consider the following questions.

- *What went well?*
- *What didn't go so well?*
- *When things didn't go well, how did you respond?*
- *What did you enjoy and would like to build on in future?*
- *What didn't you enjoy and would like to avoid in future?*

Single points of failure

When trying to understand office politics and why some people got promoted, whilst others who appeared to work harder and were always busy didn't, I noticed the principle of being 'too busy to promote'.

Regardless of justification, management may see some people as fulfilling a role so successfully that to remove them would result in an unacceptable level of adjustment for the business. These people are essentially punished for their hard work, but also for becoming a single point of failure and over-reliance.

I've also worked with contractors whose aim was to make themselves so ingrained in the business that the client had 'no choice' but to extend their contract.

After this realization, even when I was employed, I never looked to get too embedded with any product or process. Equally, as a contractor, my first thought was always how I could hand over my role to the client's regular team, and essentially make myself redundant.

With that approach, it's amazing how often I was kept on and offered more valuable work, whereas contractors who had tried to keep information to themselves were given a short window to hand over their knowledge then leave.

Single points of failure are detrimental to businesses and personal growth.

The same applies as you're looking to grow your business. It may only be you, but the more you can remove the reliance on yourself as a single point of failure, the stronger your business will be. This will enable you to work *on* your business, not *in* it.

If you're eventually looking to sell the business, the less reliant it is on you, the more valuable it will be.

Action 5J

Put a process in place to review and monitor how much time you're spending on rather than in your business. Put in targets to ensure time spent on your business increases, therefore reducing its reliance on you. Capture any single points of failure and put in steps to eradicate them.

Self-care

As your business takes off – or worse, if it doesn't – the likelihood is that you'll continue to have more and more things to do within your working day.

As part of your checkpoint reviews, take the time to consider your own health and whether you're keeping to the time you made for non-work and rewarding yourself, as covered in Step 4: Undertake.

In 'Early priorities' in Step 4: Undertake, we looked at the Pareto Principle – that 80% of the benefit comes from 20% of the effort. That is equally true here and, after applying it, if you still feel you need to do more than you probably should, look at what you can outsource, automate or simply stop.

It may not be work alone that burns you out, but also other responsibilities in your life such as childcare or looking after elderly relatives. It adds up to the same result.

Keeping an eye on the time you make for exercise, healthy eating and your personal sleep needs is always a good thing, but especially when you're super-busy. These are the essentials of self-care. But it takes more than this to thrive.

Communications expert Sara Price explains the immense value of self-care.

A lot of entrepreneurs struggle with self-care and the first step towards a healthier approach is to identify, explore and challenge the limiting beliefs that you have about what self-care means. Here are two common examples.

Limiting belief 1: 'I don't have time to take care of myself'

I hear this a lot, but is it really true? When my clients on the edge of burnout tell me that they don't have time to take a break, that right now isn't convenient, I ask them a simple question: what's more inconvenient – taking five days off now or being forced to take five months off in a few months' time?

When we say we don't have time, what we're really saying is, 'this isn't a priority for me right now'. If our own self-care was a priority, we'd find the time.

Limiting belief 2: 'Self-care is selfish'

Purpose-led entrepreneurs looking to make a difference in the world really suffer from this. They often believe that taking time out for themselves is selfish because their purpose is to be of service to others.

Here's the thing: your vision is unique, and only you can deliver it. So, if you burn out, who is going to fulfil your unique purpose?

I understand that you don't want to worry the people around you. But do you honestly think that those who care about you aren't already worried? And when you do burn out, it'll be those people – your friends and family – who have to pick up the pieces and take care of you. So not only will you be unable to fulfil your purpose and be of service to others; you'll actually need to be cared for by the very people you are trying to protect.

When you think about it that way, maybe not taking care of yourself is more selfish than self-care.

I asked Sara her best tip on implementing self-care.

Once you've sorted out your beliefs you need to work out what self-care actually looks like for you.

For years I would read books and listen to self-care 'gurus' and try to adopt the routines they suggested. I tried morning rituals, meditation, yoga, journaling, scheduling in micro-breaks every hour and so on. Within a few days, I'd fail to keep up with my new routine and end up berating myself for not taking care of myself as I was supposed to.

Eventually I worked out that self-care is different for everybody, and what works for you won't necessarily work for me.

Sara now takes what she calls a 'care and curiosity month' twice each year. This is time completely away from work that she uses, in her own words, 'to replenish, relax, read and explore'. That still leaves ten months of the year to deliver on her purpose.

Think in detail about each of those four words, and you'll see that they enable body and mind to refuel, to offer more as a result. I absolutely see the value in why Sara does this, and consider it an investment rather than a holiday.

Action 5K

Identify and explore the limiting beliefs you have, and strongly challenge yourself about them. Work out what self-care means for you: what your needs are, what works for you and how you achieve it. Make a commitment to prioritize those needs.

- *How will you refuel?*
- *What is necessary for you at a basic level, and what will enable you to thrive?*

Extraordinary Steering Meeting

An Extraordinary Steering Meeting is a Steering Meeting outside of the normal cycle. It may be needed as a decision-making forum with the input of your SteerCo in the following circumstances:

- to put in place a plan to resolve a significant issue
- to consider a new opportunity that may expand the business or significantly change your goals or objectives

- to respond to a threat from a new regulation or a competitor for which you have to take urgent and decisive action
- to consider moving through a gate or into a new phase

The final reason could be simply when you've decided your business has reached a steady state – business-as-usual (BAU) – having delivered on your Phase 2 plan. This is when you feel ready to move into Phase 3 and expand at whatever level is right for you and your business.

As with all Steering Meetings, ensure you have a strong, clear agenda specifying the recommendations and what justifies that course of action.

Retrospective

As you reach the end of Step 5: Review, you should be confident you know when to step in and take a closer look at each aspect of your business – be it strategic direction, the performance of a key supplier, customer feedback or even the suitability of a freelancer you use *ad hoc*.

Early intervention is key, as is open and honest feedback. Your reviews should absolutely be in sync with how you're delivering on your business objectives, and you should be able to utilize both gate and checkpoint reviews as a result.

We covered a range of tools, techniques and considerations to enable you to review successfully.

Finally, we looked at when you might need the advice of your SteerCo beyond your regular meeting rhythm.

Once your business is stable, your Phase 2 objectives have been met and you've aligned with your SteerCo, it'll be time to pass through the gate.

Let's start making it better!

Phase 3
Making it better

Initiating Phase 3

Phase 3 is about making it better. Once you've made it happen and built your business, the next step is to make it work for you, and continuously improve it.

Phase 3 consists of the sixth and final step of the FUTURE Method. This is as follows.

- Step 6: Expand to the next adventure, taking in all the experiences and lessons from what has come before.

Phase 3 can be considered the start of business-as-usual (BAU); however, as we'll learn, it's often anything but!

When you've completed the actions in Phase 3, you should be clear on your options for expanding your business, and to ensure it continues to work for you.

Before that, though, it's time to think about your plan again.

Plan

The Phase 3 plan is an interesting one because it isn't easy to define.

You're likely to use the following sub-steps as a basis for workstreams that are more standalone, or on a separate timeframe to much of what we've covered so far. You may have other priorities you'd like to bring in beyond the scope of what I cover here, including some objectives to achieve your long-term goals.

In terms of duration, if you had Phase 2 as a minimum six-month plan, I suggest that Phase 3 is at least a further 12 months. Whilst some of the sub-steps will be workstreams within your plan until they're implemented, others will be ongoing considerations that will need regular effort assigned for the duration of your time with the business or until you close down those initiatives.

How and when you baseline the Phase 3 plan will also depend on the duration you choose, and the regularity of your planning cycles. It could be that this is when your approach becomes more aligned with an agile way of working.

To do this, you'd create a backlog of requirements for everything you want to complete in this phase of the project. They are grouped, sized and prioritized as normal. The highest priority – or most appropriate to be delivered by the team you have available – are then brought forward, in line with your capacity, to deliver as part of a time-limited process commonly called a sprint.

To retain control of delivery, a sprint should be no longer than four weeks. You could also plan and baseline all the sprints within a quarterly planning cycle at once, for example.

Step 6: Expand

The scope

If Step 5: Review was the parallel step to Step 4: Undertake, Step 6: Expand is its heir. In this step you'll discover a range of options for expanding your business.

Just like in Step 4: Undertake, there are some fabulous contributions here from some very talented subject matter experts, and also those who have been through the journey themselves.

It can be easy to sit back, but business never stands still. The deeper you get into your business, the more you'll find comes your way. That may result in a further pivot, partnerships or even closing down things that are successful.

Let's start expanding!

Close and learn

In a standard project, this is the point where the project manager would look to close down the project, capture the lessons learned for next time and formally move it into BAU.

Looking back to 'Building or maintaining' in Step 2: Understand, in a technology environment this is where the teams responsible for maintaining the offering in BAU start to get interested, and those responsible for building it (who often manage the early life support once the project goes live) start to disband and move on to the next project.

This is far from the end of your story, however, as this is the time to expand your business into whatever you want it to be going forward.

Your regular reviews should have given you insight into what is going well, what isn't going so well and some opportunities you can follow up on to make your business better as it becomes a little more normal.

You'll need to decide which of the review forums you keep, and their cadence. It may be that you reduce the frequency of some of them.

Action 6A

At a high level, consider how you'll look to expand your business and set appropriate goals. Think about the structure and cadence of your reviews and ensure you maintain what will best serve you and your business.

Is 'do nothing' an option?

Before expanding your business in any form, it's worth considering if you want to. You may be happy with your lot, having created a business that works well for yourself and your family and feel like there is no need to change.

If that's the case, brilliant! However, it's worth remembering that things rarely stay still in business (or, indeed, in life), and if you remain static it may be that your competitors catch up or new ones enter the market and begin to dilute your market share. Alternatively, your customers may no longer need your solution and may not be replaced by new ones.

In this scenario, it's worth keeping a close eye on your business to ensure it is delivering consistently. Trends of reduced sales without mitigating action being taken can result in a slow and painful decline.

Action 6B

If you're happy to have a consistent business that suits your lifestyle, work out ways you can keep it fresh, and keep a close eye on sales trends to see if your customers agree.

The contribution equation

> *Every time you meet an objective, you realize there is still more to be achieved.*

These are the words of psychologist and entrepreneur Lynda Holt. I couldn't agree more, and it would be funny if it wasn't so true.

A key part of what to consider when you expand is the contribution you'll make by doing so, and the satisfaction you'll get from it. Put in a simple equation, the contribution you'll make by doing something has to be bigger than the cost, or effort, required to achieve it. Lynda explains.

> *If you settle for where you are now, what will it feel like inside? Will there be something more that you haven't given?*

> *If you're clear it makes a difference, you're clear on the direction of your business and have a burning desire to take it forward but don't do it, then you may never feel settled or successful. There will be something missing at a human level by not fulfilling what is important to you.*

In 'Getting comfortable with feeling uncomfortable' in Step 3: Trial, we covered developing a growth mindset. In many ways, I see this as an expansion of that, but it's about more than personal growth or even achieving business goals. It's using your business as a vehicle for the contribution you want to make.

Lynda explains how she has utilized this approach.

I've always had a ten-year-out vision of what impact I'd like to make. It isn't about business goals, because business changes much more quickly than that, but the vision and the impact haven't really changed because it's part of who I am. I help people to be courageous enough to do what makes a difference to them.

The way I've delivered it has changed over time but being aware of my contribution has helped as I've grown, risked breaking it and took it to the next scary step. My mission is bigger than being comfortable, and I always choose contribution over comfort, because in the end that's what makes me feel successful.

Action 6C

Be clear on what is driving you.

- *As you expand your business, how can you improve the contribution you make?*
- *What does success mean to you?*
- *What will make you satisfied?*
- *How can you weave your contribution into your business?*

Pivot again

When looking to expand your business, it could be that you pivot again.

I stayed steady for the first five years of my business, making only minor adjustments to the type of services I offered. This was due to a combination of factors. They were mainly personal reasons, but I was also enjoying the work I was doing with corporate clients. I also hadn't worked out how I could pivot to the next step or how my lifestyle needs would require the business to adjust.

Once you've lived your business for a while and grown with it, one way or another you'll find the experience differs from what you had in mind.

Even if it's everything you wanted it to be, as we covered when considering the 'do nothing' option, it may be that your market moves, or your circumstances change.

Action 6D

Take the time to reflect on the journey you've been on and consider where, if anywhere, you should pivot to next. Revisit the INPUTS Business Case Framework and Phase 1 more generally to help with considering your options. Ask yourself the following.

- *What doors have opened?*
- *What doors have closed?*
- *Are you happy that the doors have closed?*
- *Have you gone down the wrong path and need to backtrack?*
- *Who have you met who has changed your thinking about your business and what you should do next?*
- *How have your values changed?*
- *How have your personal circumstances changed?*
- *How has your market changed?*
- *What feedback have you received from customers you could act upon?*
- *Ignoring everything you've built in your business, if you could start again what itch would you scratch now?*

Natural expansion

It may be that you don't want to pivot, and you're perfectly happy with the direction of your business. This doesn't stop the opportunity to expand, however. In many ways, it keeps it simpler and gives you options you can more easily assess.

There are several strategies you can use to expand your business whilst staying on the same track.

Simplest of all, you could *improve your reach* with your current customer profile and grow your market share.

If you're keeping your existing offering, you could expand into a *new geography* or sell via a *new marketplace*.

You could tweak your products or services so they appeal to a *new demographic* within your market or even to a *new market in a different industry*.

You could also create *complementary products or services* in order to increase your presence in your current market and sell more to your current customers – as I've mentioned, these are always the easiest people to sell something to.

Fine jewellery aficionado Trang Do explains how she expanded by offering a new service.

> *I'd heard so many stories from men saying they did their research and bought an expensive jewellery gift, and then she didn't want it. So, I created a service called 'BBeyond', short for 'be beyond expectation'.*
>
> *It's designed to deliver a unique gifting experience. It's fun and convenient for the person buying the gift, and unforgettable for the person receiving it.*
>
> *They want to present an amazing, personalized gift and experience but are short of time and lacking in original ideas. They fill in a short questionnaire, why they're buying the gift, who it's for and what, if anything, they have in mind. We send a list of suggestions and invite them on a call to explore further and find an option that will delight them both.*
>
> *For a deposit, we then create two designs that can be presented on the special occasion, via a personalized greetings card or a framed picture. Many women like to make the final decision on such personal items, so our solution shows the effort and creates an experience, but without the risk of them being disappointed by the result.*
>
> *We can also arrange extra touches to make the occasion perfect. The whole thing is about the experience, and those memories will be forever associated with the final piece.*

This example utilizes the *new demographic* and *complementary service* strategies, with the result being a wider appeal of Trang's core product.

Additionally, it utilizes a *complementary products* strategy with options available to maximize the experience for her customers.

Action 6E

Consider how you could expand using each of these strategies, or a combination of them. If several options could work for you, prioritize them.

Your book and podcast

However you choose to take your business forward, more people becoming aware of you will improve the visibility of your business and lead to more sales.

As we've covered when looking at both social media and PR, a key way to increase awareness is to publish. So how about publishing your own book or even creating your own podcast?

Even during the writing phase of this book, my network has increased significantly, and I've received a lot of goodwill from others as a result.

Speaking to people who have been through the journey and published their books, there are common themes of the unexpected routes the book can take and the opportunities it can create.

Parenting coach Elaine Halligan is the author of *My Child's Different*. She explains the impact the book has had.

> *The impact both personally and for the business has taken us by surprise. I think a book, if it's well written and well edited, can be incredible collateral. Parenting is deeply personal and from reading the book readers feel a deeper connection to you and your offering.*

> *It has helped us expand to reach a larger audience of schools and teachers, corporates and working parents, and also to establish a premium brand as leading parenting education providers globally.*

Behavioural skills specialist Chris Watson, author of *Upskill: 21 Keys to Professional Growth*, agrees.

Writing a book has really helped to raise the profile of my business. For example, there has been a tangible increase in bookings for a stand-alone programme called 'Unexpected Ways to Develop Yourself and Others' which deliberately mirrors many of the themes inside the book.

The traction created by the book encourages you to put yourself out there, which in turn can lead to so many new opportunities. With the book in print and the publicity around it, you become far more accessible to people after they've heard you talking.

But, I hear you ask, 'what would I write a book about?' Your journey, like all of ours, is unique and sharing the story of the obstacles you've overcome, or your approach, will undoubtedly add value for some-body – just like hopefully I have for you.

It's also a great conversation-starter. It will give you credibility with prospective customers and is the strongest business card you could ever hand over.

From my own writing journey, I also think the deep thought required during the writing process can provide clarity for your business and the direction in which you want to take it.

In terms of a podcast, this offers its own immense value. Podcasts are becoming more popular because they are so flexible. Being audio-only, listeners can often multi-task without missing out on content, and can listen whilst commuting, cooking, exercising and so on.

Elaine explains how this developed for her.

Following the book, The Parent Practice Podcast *has also emerged, so the opportunities to reach global audiences has never been so exciting.*

A podcast will grow your network and potential customer base both through the guests you have and the listeners you attract. If your guests have a significant profile, people will become aware of you as a result.

My experience was similar to Elaine's, as the interviews I conducted with the contributors for this book were the spark that led to *The Project Future Podcast.* Those interviews absolutely showed me the value in sharing the journey of others with a specific focus, which in my case is the initial journey of starting a business and overcoming challenges to make it a success.

Before starting a podcast, consider becoming a guest on somebody else's. I'm always open to being a podcast guest as this can be powerful for visibility, potentially opening you up to a whole new audience. It's also lots of fun.

Action 6F

Consider the theme of your own book and podcast. Start talking to people about the prospect and consider their feedback. If now isn't the right time, work out when it will be and put it on your three-year plan. Engage with others and be a guest on their podcast. Finally, listen to The Project Future Podcast *and see what inspiration you can get from my guests.*

Closing down successful products or services

Sometimes it's necessary to close down a product or service, even if it's profitable and has been successful.

It may sound counter-intuitive, but just because it has worked in the past doesn't mean it will work in the future.

Even if it does work in the future, it may not be aligned to your strategy going forward, having fulfilled its purpose, or it may be taking up more of your energy than it's worth and doesn't justify adding somebody to your team to cover it. Alternatively, it may simply be that you don't enjoy it enough to justify the continued investment or it's no longer aligned to your values or mission.

Whichever of the above is true, in order to keep your business lean and looking forward you should be willing to pull the plug, remember the good times and move onwards and upwards.

As covered earlier, when tech entrepreneur Paul Hulligan started his independent career he took any freelance work available, and this led to a successful freelance partnership where he was an assistant to an experienced filmmaker. Paul enjoyed this work – it was regular and fairly lucrative – but as his own filmmaking company grew, he decided to scale it back as he didn't have the bandwidth and headspace for both.

Such a change doesn't have to be permanent. If you find the opportunity you wanted to focus on doesn't give the results you hoped for, there is always the option to go back. If you've built strong connections and scaled something back or closed it down for the right reasons in a professional, courteous way, people who you've worked with previously or your previous customers could be open to restarting.

Think about what legacy work you've been known for during your time as an employee. It may be that you've been promoted since, or simply moved on to bigger and better things, but there are always people that will remember you for something; they know you'll do a solid job and will get in touch hoping you'll do it for them. It's the same principle here. Your focus should always be on the future and what will shape your business the way you want to shape it.

Action 6G

Evaluate when your products or services will reach the end of their useful life. Consider if there is any value in outsourcing or selling them to another company. If not, decide if it's time to say 'thanks for the memories' and move on.

Collaborations and partnerships

Building on 'Outsourcing' from Step 2: Understand, as you expand consider how collaborations and partnerships can work for your business. They can come in all different shapes and sizes, but all are designed to increase your reach and improve what you offer your customers.

There is a partnership where you literally have a partner, or partners, and *share equity* in the business with them (covered in Step 2: Understand), but it's much more nuanced than that.

Every *supplier* you engage can be considered a partner, whether they're providing physical products as part of your supply chain or whether they're running your social media accounts, for example.

You can set up *affiliate programmes*, where others promote your business for a set commission on the sales they generate. This is another area technology has simplified in recent years.

There are also partnerships, where you work with a *complementary business* to advocate their services to your customers, and in turn they recommend their customers to you. This arrangement may be formal or informal.

You may also *collaborate* with another business or individual to generate a product that wouldn't be possible by either party alone.

As we touched on in 'The sales factor' in Pre-step 2, competition isn't necessarily negative, and could provide an option for you to collaborate or partner. A competitor could have a complementary offering or overlap with your offering, and working together could benefit you, your competitor and your customers.

People can also be willing to refer a customer to another business if they think it's a better fit for them.

Communications expert Sara Price explains her approach.

> *I start from the position that I want to offer the best possible service to my clients. Implicit in that is the understanding that sometimes the best service isn't going to be mine – or at least not mine alone. Collaboration is key to this, and from the outset of my first business, over ten years ago, we've had partners that we referred projects to and collaborators that we brought on-board to deliver specialist work for our clients.*

> *In my second business I've followed the same approach. I have a group of 'Actually Partners' who offer services that are complementary to mine, and I not only refer work to them – I actively promote them to my clients and collaborate with them on everything from masterclasses to masterminds.*

Whatever the relationship with your collaborators and partners, ensure that you share some values, that your agreement is balanced and that both parties are entering into it with the right intent.

Do your research before signing up to any formal arrangements as getting it wrong can be painful. Getting it right, however, can significantly expand the reach of your business and further delight your customers.

Action 6H

Draw up a roadmap of potential collaborations and partnerships.

- *Could you involve some of your competitors?*
- *How could this benefit and delight your customers?*

Focusing on your priorities

Opportunities come along all the time. They may not appear obvious, but they are there – and have been throughout your career. The trick is knowing which ones to say 'yes' to and, as importantly, when to say 'no'.

In 'Abundance' in Step 4: Undertake, I gave several reasons why you should consider giving things away, and the message here shouldn't be confused with that. Sharing is great, but it should be strategic, and it should have limits.

An opportunity you should seriously consider will provide all of the following.

- It will be aligned with your goals and values.
- There will be something in it for you.
- It will take up a proportionate amount of your time based on the value the opportunity brings.

Saying 'yes' to opportunities that don't meet these criteria means that the right opportunities may not find the space to appear, and ultimately block your growth.

If the opportunity doesn't feel right, it's perfectly acceptable to politely decline.

If things go well, this is a challenge you'll encounter more and more. Parenting coach Elaine Halligan shares her advice and experience.

It's ok to say no. My top tip would be to protect your time and be honourable to your own priorities.

I think in the early days, and even now to some extent, we are loath to say no, as I am always curious and open to all conversations. We are a very collaborative organization and every day we have people wanting to collaborate with us, to deliver shared workshops, but that's not how collaboration works.

Collaboration works by finding out about the other person's business first, by developing meaningful relationships. Recently, an author wrote to me asking if I would be happy to be interviewed for his book. I replied saying I would need to see a copy of the manuscript first as he was unknown to me. He responded saying he respected my decision, and this had made him reassess his approach.

We received so many cold emails, and in the early days we were too willing to help, and not strategic enough in our responses. In doing so it hijacked my time.

In this scenario, it can be easy to go off-message or lose focus on your priorities, lose focus on your customers or simply run out of time in the day. Elaine concludes.

You can do anything, but you can't do everything, and you can't help everyone.

Action 6I

Decide in what circumstances you'll be willing to say yes to collaboration, where you should ask for more information, and where you should respectfully say no, staying true to your own priorities.

Competitions and awards

Applying for competitions or awards may not be an obvious objective for you. Being judged publicly can bring discomfort and fear of failure, but it can be an excellent way to gain an edge over your competitors and to increase your credibility. You may also grow your network and attract investors as a result of winning or applying for a competition or award. This is, in its own way, a form of marketing.

We saw when we covered 'Real-world experience' in Step 3: Trial how tech entrepreneur Paul Hulligan used starting a competition to fast-forward his filmmaking social enterprise. But Paul also applied for a competition, which resulted in an acceleration of his wedding films company and significantly increased its profile. Paul explains.

> *As an alumnus of the University of East London, my business partner received an email about a competition it was running. The prize was £6,000 grant money and office space for a year. We decided to go for it, and it definitely gave us an incentive and pushed the business forward quicker than we'd planned.*
>
> *About 90 start-ups applied, a mix of students and alumni. The commitment was to attend weekly evening workshops for three months. It went through several stages where we had to pitch to get through to the next stage. We got to the top ten, then the top five, and then we had to pitch our plan to a panel of experienced entrepreneurs at a grand final event in Canary Wharf. We won it!*

Despite the success, Paul gives a word of warning.

> *It was a lot of work to get there. You could argue we put more than £6,000 worth of our own time and effort into winning the competition! You've got to be sure it's the right time for you to apply, as to make it worthwhile you need to put the effort in.*

That wasn't the end of the story. Paul concludes.

> *That success gave us an appetite for investment and also the know-how of what investors look for, so we started looking at other opportunities. We've looked at angel investment, venture capitalists and have now secured a significant investment from an investment company under the UK Seed Enterprise Investment Scheme (SEIS) which should really help to drive the business forward.*

In addition to applying for awards and competitions, there are ways you can support those that already exist, either as a judge or another form of contribution. Or why not consider starting your own?

Whatever your niche, there is every chance there is a gap where others would be grateful for the opportunity to apply for an award or competition you can create. They don't need to be global or even national awards; you could start with your niche within your local area as a focal point, for example.

When publicizing the awards, you could attract sponsors that wish to be associated with the event and therefore cover some of the costs or provide the prizes. As long as it's delivered well, this kind of event will lead to people thinking favourably of you as an authority within your field.

Action 6J

- *What competitions and awards can you apply for to increase the profile and visibility of your business?*
- *What competition or awards can you create?*
- *If you want it, how can this be a springboard to invest-ment?*

Growing your team

There may come a time when outsourcing of specific tasks is no longer enough, and you need more substantial support in the form of a team.

When you're considering growing your team, you have several options. Employment regulations will vary depending on where you're based, so we won't go into this too deeply, but in general the following applies.

- Full-time, part-time, fixed-term contracts and apprentice-ships have an employment contract.
- Freelancers, limited company contractors, agency contrac-tors, volunteers and interns don't have an employment contract.

Growing your team should allow you to focus on the value-adding stuff like strategy, gaining new customers, retaining the ones you have and improving what you offer them – working *on* your business, not *in* it, and thus removing the single point of failure we covered in Step 5: Review.

To evolve without a team around you becomes a risk in itself as there just isn't the time in the day to do everything justice.

As we covered elsewhere in Step 5: Review, detailed forecasting will allow you to plan for the needs of your business, including capacity planning.

With improvements to technology in recent years, it's absolutely possible to grow a team around you in a flexible way. People often don't need to physically be in the same place or work set hours. Business levels and needs also vary, and that's where the option to outsource to freelancers could be the right solution. Equally, if you partner with another business you may increase the services they manage over time.

If you're working with freelancers, in particular, the relationship may be different from when you've managed staff previously. Due to often being in different places, clear communication is key. Freelancers often value the flexibility in their lifestyle, so give them sufficient detail on what you're expecting from them, and by when you want it completed. It's not your concern where they are and what time of day it is when they complete the work. As long as it's done by the deadline to the quality required by you and your customers, everyone will be happy.

Once you get to a certain workload consistently, however, you may get the confidence to employ a permanent member of staff instead.

Action 6K

Think about when and how you can expand your team.

- *How can you get maximum value and free up your own time, whilst keeping the risks low?*
- *What measures will you use to determine when the right time is to bring on board your first employee?*

Training your team

However you choose to grow your team, they'll need to be trained. In 'Ways of working' in Step 4: Undertake, we covered how you can capture your one way of completing tasks, making them simple, logical and repeatable and recording them in 'How To' guides, preferably in video format.

Showing your 'How To' videos to your new team when you expand will allow you to share your message in a controlled way, with less effort required on your part. This is a classic win–win.

Builder of sale-ready businesses Marianne Page explains the pitfalls that often happen if a business hasn't systemized its tasks.

> As the business grows and new team members join, they are taught by people who have their own preferred way of doing things and everything unravels in terms of consistency.
>
> There is often a misconception that training takes place in the first week or two after somebody joins, and then they just get on with the role, but that's not the case. Every team member goes on a whole learning journey that starts on Day 1 and doesn't end until the day they leave the business. Mapping the whole learning journey for each role in the business is a vital process.

Marianne suggests asking yourself the following questions.

- *What does somebody need to know in their first week?*
- *Do we have the 'How To' guides for each task?*
- *What do they then need to learn in their first 90 days?*
- *Do we have the 'How To' guides for each task?*
- *How are we going to track what they're learning?*

Marianne continues.

> A common complaint from business owners is that nobody follows the processes they've spent time creating. Creating them is one thing; taking the time to train your team to follow them is another.
>
> For small teams, a simple spreadsheet works well. For larger teams of six or more, consider a training tracker that can act as both a container for your 'How To' guides and a tool for tracking who has been trained on what.

Once you have your 'How To' guides and your training system in place you're able to remove yourself from this process, confident that your team is following your one right way. If you appear in the 'How

To' videos, your new team members also get a feeling they're getting to know you via these videos, without you having to physically be there or continually repeat the same things. This is vital if your team are working remotely. It's also a scalable solution.

Action 6L

Map the learning journey for each role in your business and the next roles you think may be needed, regardless of how light-touch they are. Develop your training tracker and fill any gaps in the 'How To' guides.

Creating assets

The more assets you create, the more income you can generate and the more your business will be worth.

Documented processes and 'How To' guides are assets. Products are assets. Digital tools are assets. Structured services with names and specific deliverables are assets. The staff that drive a business forward are assets (freelancers, on the other hand, may not contribute to the value of a business in the same way).

This is the first and only place you'll see passive income mentioned in this book, as it's simply something I don't believe in.

You could argue I'll receive passive income from sales of this book well after I've finished writing it, but the reality is if I don't put the work in to market it – continuously – sales will reduce then stop altogether.

Equally, we have friends who have sold their buy-to-let properties as their supposed low-maintenance investment turned out to be anything but.

My approach is to use the cash reserves you have available to create assets aligned to your own skill set and interests that will continue to provide an income for your business for years ahead, and also increase its valuation.

Action 6M

Do an inventory check of the assets you have today, either fully complete or in progress.

- *How can you 'sweat the assets' to make the most of them?*

Create an assets roadmap of what you can create going forward to continue making your business stronger.

Scaling your business

Thinking back to when I was a 14-year-old schoolboy beginning to learn about business and economics, the first thing I remember being taught was economies of scale. According to this concept, dating back to Adam Smith in the eighteenth century, the higher the volume, the lower the costs per unit become, and therefore the profit margin per unit increases.

This isn't restricted to large-scale manufacturing, however.

Scaling the parts of your business that can scale will allow you to make the most of the resources you have available.

When you're creating assets, design them, and the processes that support them, so that they scale. If you do this, as you attract more customers, your costs won't go up significantly, but your opportunity to earn revenue does. Therefore, the profit margin per unit increases.

This also works for services. You can create something once for a customer, then modify it for future customers rather than starting from scratch each time.

Setting up 'one right way' to complete each task and creating 'How To' guides are excellent examples of foundations for beginning to scale your offering. It's the platform for growing your team and training them in how to deliver consistently and therefore enabling you to increase your capacity and capabilities.

Scaling can also provide an opportunity to focus on improving other aspects of your business, conversely by reducing margins. As optimist and entrepreneur Sam Halligan's business expanded, he brought on board a business partner and took on a warehouse where his cars are stored and given sympathetic restoration. Sam explains.

My focus now is on optimizing the business and scaling it. In terms of positioning the business, we focus on being highly credible. Transparency is key as customers don't often physically see the product, so we look to offer an exceptional service. The service uplift has reduced our margins, but we're looking to compensate that with scale.

But not all parts of a business can scale. There is only one of you, and although you can make training videos, you can't use this digital substitute of yourself to provide feedback to your team, plan your strategy or meet with potential customers, so consider the real value-adding activities that justify the repeat effort when thinking about what, and how, to scale.

Action 6N

- *What parts of your proposition are repeatable for multiple customers?*
- *What capabilities will be required to enable your business to work at scale?*
- *What other aspects could you improve if lower margins were compensated by scale?*

Work out what areas of the business you cannot scale and where an extra, personal touch is justified.

Exit plan

It may seem out of place in a book about starting a business, but now we're going to look at an exit plan. One way or another, your time in the business will come to an end.

You may not wish this to happen any time soon, but it's worth keeping in mind and preparing for nevertheless. Your circumstances could change, or another opportunity may come up that you'd like capital to invest in as your next adventure.

If you plan it well, this could be a profitable sale and justification for the work you've put in to build the business assets, customer base, team, supply chain, processes and systems.

If you don't plan it well, or at all, it could result in a simple liquidation and closure of the business.

As we've covered, the more tangible assets you have in the business, and the freer it is to run without depending on your presence, the higher the valuation will likely be.

Selling a business is remarkably similar to selling a house, and the same professions are involved: solicitors, accountants and agents (known as business transfer agents). Also, like selling a house, it can take a while to find the right buyer, so having all paperwork in place is a must to speed the process up.

During my years in M&A, I was involved in a variety of exits, where the roles of the key stakeholders differed as a result of the sale. It's possible to stay on in a new role, stay on for a defined period or exit upon completion, and this will vary based not only on your own preference but in agreement with the buyer.

Also, the type of transaction can vary. Your company could merge with a rival or complementary company, be acquired by a larger company (or, in some circumstances, a smaller one), you could sell to an individual or group that wishes to take it, which may be external or within your staff, or you could even sell shares in the company via an initial public offering (IPO).

There is likely to be an optimum time for you to sell, when the valuation and your desire to exit meet, so I suggest keeping this in mind as an option within your strategic planning cycle. It may be that your expansion is to say goodbye.

Action 6O

Consider when the optimum time may be to sell or exit from the business and build it into your plan as necessary. Seek insight from business transfer agents who will be able to advise you on market conditions, an estimated valuation and any objectives you could deliver that would improve the valuation ahead of putting the business on the market.

Retrospective

As you reach the end of Step 6: Expand – and indeed the end of the six-step FUTURE Method – you should now be clear on a range of options for expanding your business.

As well as expanding your business, it's about keeping yourself fresh and energized. Your business is there to work for you, not the other way around, and therefore if you decide that any element of it – or indeed the whole thing – has served its purpose then that's absolutely your prerogative. The decision to close or exit is yours.

Congratulations on getting to the end of the six steps! Are you clear on your next steps and the journey ahead?

Let's look at bringing it all together.

A bright FUTURE

Applying the FUTURE Method

The six-step FUTURE Method was designed to help you develop and deliver a plan, bringing structure and accountability.

Each of the six steps we've been through adds value in its own way. It simply wouldn't work without one of them, or if done in the wrong order.

I intuitively followed the method during every step of my early career as I progressed from job to job, and then from contract to contract after I set up my own business. But I didn't realize it at the time.

Having been working on the model and fleshing it out for a considerable amount of time, I now simply wouldn't contemplate deciding to make a significant investment of time, money or energy without completing the first three steps and then having a solid plan to both make it happen (Steps 4 and 5) and make it better (Step 6).

I hope this also applies to you, and you can see the model working for you on your own adventures.

What you discovered

In the Introduction, I made a big promise – that this book would empower aspiring entrepreneurs, freelancers and contractors to ask themselves the right questions at the right stage to give them the best chance of getting their independent career off the ground and making it a success.

I said that by following my process, 'that' person could be you. I hope that person *is* now you.

I hope you can now apply key project management techniques just like big business does.

I hope your mindset is now in a place where you can set a goal and make it a reality.

I hope you now have the tools and the confidence to make decisions that are appropriate to your own unique skills, interests and circumstances.

I hope you can now make a plan that focuses on delivering your priorities.

I hope you're now comfortable taking on and managing the right level of risk for you.

I hope you can now review your progress and can take steps to expand to the next level.

I hope poor decisions or deciding not to consider a change – things that can result in years of unfulfillment, missed opportunities and regret – are now strictly off the menu.

Finally, I hope you're now in a position to think strategically, and that you're empowered to make sound decisions and be bold and in control of your future.

Be confident and have no regrets

You may have reached the end of this book and still have doubts that being your own boss isn't for you, or fears that you don't have what it takes to succeed. If that's the case, my advice is to look at the evidence.

What is concerning you the most? If you have imposter syndrome and the thought of taking a controlled risk feels too much, or if you're a natural introvert like me and the thought of going public terrifies you, then fight back against that 'survival' instinct in your head and demand more.

You deserve more than you've got today. If you've followed the steps in this book and got sign-off at each gating decision then you've proved you can make a plan to succeed, whatever success means to you.

If you haven't started yet, start today and have no regrets.

I wish you every success on your journey.

A final action:
Don't be a stranger

I'd be delighted to know what you thought of the book and how you see it working for you.

What have you named your project and what is your goal as an outcome of it?

I'd also love to see where in the world you are, so feel free to post a photo of the book (with yourself, if you'd like) and your location with any feedback tagging @robkerrauthor on Instagram.

If you haven't done so already, from my website (www.robkerr.co.uk) you can complete a short quiz to discover your strengths and areas to improve as you prepare to start your journey.

From my website you can also see what appearances I'm making, and find out how to work with me to delve deeper, either one-to-one or in a group, into some of the themes introduced in this book. This is where I'll work with you to drive better decision-making, launch the right business for you or make your business better.

I work with both individuals directly and through an employer, offering a range of outplacement services.

If you leave a verified review on whatever platform through which you bought the book, it will help to spread the knowledge and give more people the clarity and confidence to launch their own brilliant business. Or be old-school and just talk about it!

About the author

Rob Kerr is a crackerjack at asking questions. His project management career has laid the foundations for asking questions that align to his true purpose – working with aspiring and new business owners to drive better decision-making and create better businesses that solve the problems they care about.

Rob is the creator of the *FUTURE Method*, an innovative and contemporary approach to planning and starting a business. He is the host of *The Project Future Podcast*, where his guests share their insights and experiences from starting their own businesses, and he chairs *The Project Future Club* group on Facebook.

Photograph by Daniel Herendi

Away from business, Rob loves to run and often builds a half-marathon into a cheeky weekend break. He is originally from Essex and lives in London with his wife and two children.

Find him and get in touch.

Website www.robkerr.co.uk
Email hello@robkerr.co.uk
Facebook community www.facebook.com/groups/projectfutureclub
Instagram www.instagram.com/robkerrauthor
LinkedIn www.linkedin.com/in/robkerrauthor

About the contributors

As the founder of the award-winning Endor Learn & Develop, **Chris Watson** specializes in the promotion of adaptive management practices. Incurably curious about all aspects of organizational behaviour, his goal is to strengthen relationships in the workplace by sharing straightforward solutions which people can relate to on a personal level. With a proven track record in unlocking potential to help organizations flourish, Chris delivers practical ideas to extend capability and commitment.

Read his book *Upskill: 21 Keys to Professional Growth*, or contact him at www.endorlearning.com.

Dani Mosley is the founder of Family Feasts, a home cooking business based in southeast London. Dani provides cooking parties and workshops for children and families, bespoke supper clubs for special occasions and unique food gifts all year round. The business ethos is focused around bringing families back together to enjoy delicious, exciting, nutritious home-cooked food. Amongst others, Dani has had her recipes featured in *BBC Good Food* and *Co-op Food* magazines.

Dani posts regularly on Instagram (@family_feasts) and you can learn more at www.familyfeastslondon.com.

David Kerr is now semi-retired, but ran businesses in landscaping and industrial floor-laying during his career. David now spends his time on his passion for classic cars and knows a bargain when he sees one.

Elaine Halligan is the bestselling author of *My Child's Different*, a parenting coach and a school and corporate speaker, who has spent the past 12 years helping parents bring out the best in their children and find the holy grail of parenting – keeping calm. However, having raised a neurodiverse son, who was excluded from three schools by the age of seven and who has now become a budding entrepreneur, she has ridden the emotional parenting roller-coaster. Her passion is in helping parents understand their child's temperament and needs, unlock their potential and maximize their strengths. Together with business partner Melissa Hood, she helps run The Parent Practice in London.

Find out more at www.theparentpractice.com or www.linkedin.com/in/elainehalligan.

Glenn Wilson is a strategically focused DevSecOps consultant with over 20 years' experience delivering successful IT solutions across multiple industry sectors. Glenn is passionate about cybersecurity, DevSecOps and the benefits of applying secure processes and principles that augment business capabilities and enrich your relationship with your customers.

Find him on LinkedIn: www.linkedin.com/in/glennwilson or visit https://dynaminet.com.

Joanna Rawbone, MSc has run her international training and coaching consultancy since 1994. Using this experience, she has been focusing on her heart-song work, Flourishing Introverts, since 2018, enabling introverts to flourish without pretending to be something they're not. An introvert herself, Joanna also works with organizations and educational establishments to dispel the myths and surface extraversion bias with a view to enhancing wellbeing and engagement, thereby creating a more inclusive culture. Joanna's ultimate goal is to eliminate the extraversion bias, as she is only too aware of the damage it causes.

Find her at www.flourishingintroverts.com and subscribe to *The Flourishing Introvert Talks* podcast: www.flourishingintroverts.com/podcast.

Lynda Holt is an award-winning CEO of BraveScene – a development consultancy working with leaders and business owners. Over the last 19 years, she has enabled thousands of people to find the courage to do what matters to them. Lynda is the author of several books on leadership, mindset and business. Lynda is an expert in neuroscience and believes most things are possible when you get focused enough.

Find out more at www.lyndaholt.co.uk and join the Braver Business Facebook group at www.facebook.com/groups/BraveScene.

Marianne Page is an award-winning leader and developer of high-performing teams, inspiring successful small business owners to build the systems, structure and team that will free them from the day-to-day of their operation. For 27 years Marianne worked as a senior manager with McDonald's, a business built on systems, and now works with established business owners and entrepreneurs who are motivated to make their business scalable and saleable in 12 months or less. Marianne is the best-selling author of *Simple Logical Repeatable*, *The McFreedom Report*, *Process to Profit* and *Mission: To Manage*.

Visit www.mariannepage.co.uk or her Marianne Page YouTube channel.

Martin Duffy is the managing director of Majadu Ltd, an e-commerce company specializing in audiovisual accessories. Upon leaving school in 2005 he briefly worked in retail before training as an audio technician, and went full-time with his first business venture four years later. In November 2019, he released his first book, *A Clueless School-Leaver's First Decade in Business*.

Visit www.majadu.co.uk or email martin@majadu.co.uk.

Michael Young is a professional scribbler. Ever since he was a kid, he has been obsessed with putting pencil to paper and making 'scribbled sense' of the world around. He is particularly passionate about developing characters and story. That passion and obsession has evolved into his business, Family Scribbles, which provides portraits, wall art, unique gifts, book and poster illustrations services, logo and branding design, event services and much more. Michael's purpose is to connect people with people and ideas through lines, shape, colour, love and story.

See his portfolio and contact him at www.facebook.com/familyscribbles or on Instagram (@family_scribbles).

Paul Hulligan is an entrepreneur with a background in professional marketing and freelance filmmaking. He is the co-founder of Vidicrew Ltd, a video tech start-up currently disrupting the wedding market – an app and web platform which enables couples to make their own wedding film, using behind-the-scenes content captured by their loved ones of the whole wedding journey. Paul is also co-founding managing director of the London Documentary Network CIC, a social enterprise which runs events to connect the documentary film community (most notably the 36-hour filmmaking competition 'Doc in a Day').

> Find out more at www.vidicrew.com or www.linkedin.com/in/ paul-hulligan.

Ryan Edwards found the perfect home in Barcelona after living in Thailand, Australia, Cyprus and Germany. He has 15 years of leadership experience as European Marketing and Innovation Leader at Cargill and as managing director of a start-up platform for 10,000+ food experts worldwide. Now as co-founder of Naked Innovations he helps create innovative ecosystems that align planet, business and people in the agri-food industry. They challenge the status quo in the agri-food industry by empowering diverse people and focusing on openness, curiosity and fresh thinking to drive impactful, sustainable growth.

> Find out more at http://nakedinnovations.eu/ or email him at ryan@nakedinnovations.eu.

Sam Halligan is a mad proud half-Kiwi/half-Scot, with a passion for overland adventures. His dyslexia has paved the way for a varied career, ranging from event and media management to a degree in real estate. His passion for cars was ignited when, aged 17, he exported two Fiat Cinquecentos from Italy. This led to founding Samuel Lloyd & Co, where he matches worldwide petrolheads with Land Rovers and European classics. He's an avid fundraiser for the charity Cool Earth and can often be found swinging a 7-iron on a links course.

> Find out more at www.samuellloydco.com or www.linkedin.com/ in/sam-halligan.

Sara Price is an entrepreneur, coach, trainer, speaker and mentor. She's spent 25 years in communications, advising brands and organizations like Kellogg's, Avon and UNICEF. Her new venture, Actually, exists to support purpose-led entrepreneurs to unleash the power of great communications to grow their businesses and their impact. Sara helps her clients to make a difference and fulfil their purpose – that's how she fulfils hers.

> If you want to learn more about what Sara does and how she can help you, please visit www.actually.world or email talk@actually. world.

Canadian **Sophie Southmayd** began her career in Paris and now lives in London. Having worked in the beauty and fashion industries for over a decade, she has worked directly with hundreds of SMEs as well as industry giants. She launched Sophie Southmayd Consulting (Social Southmayd) in 2018, which offers digital marketing solutions and content creation for all social media platforms including Instagram and Facebook. They are social media experts who take the time to get to know a brand's ethos, creating content with the right tone of voice, all while utilizing their expertise in optics for better brand awareness.

Visit www.sophiesouthmayd.com or Instagram (@sophiesouthmayd) to find out more.

Sue Belton is an author and leadership and life coach specializing in developing ambitious professionals to lead and live by design, not default. Sue works with both organization-sponsored and private clients who want to step up and consciously design the next phase of their leadership and lives. Since 2008, hundreds of professionals have followed her unique method, which combines the principles of neuroscience, mindfulness and practical coaching techniques. Her book, *Change Your Life in 5*, was an instant sell-out on Amazon. Sue lives in London with her teenage daughter, is an advocate of early morning routines and an avid (if amateur) birdwatcher.

Find out more at www.suebelton.com or www.linkedin.com/in/suebelton.

Trang Do believes it is time to enjoy a life more meaningful, fulfilled and balanced. Having spent over a decade in the fine jewellery industry, working for some of the world's best jewellery houses, she started her own consultancy before launching her jewellery brand, Kimjoux. The business is designed around Trang's belief in the power of collaboration and empowerment. Inspired by a fresh perspective on what luxury means today, it is for the woman building her own legacy in a way that reflects her own style, personality and adventures.

Start your personal heirloom collection at www.kimjoux.com or get inspired on Instagram (@kimjoux).

Vicki Young is the personification of the 'can do' attitude, and founder of Nalla – a multi-award-winning branding agency for a fast-paced digital world. She started Nalla in 2010 at the age of 28, with the aim of ensuring the digital revolution was not ignored, and has since helped brands globally to transform. Her successes, refreshing candidness and inherent desire to innovate mean Vicki's a regular commentator on a variety of topics from business growth to branding and digital innovations. She was also awarded the title of Entrepreneur of the Year at the Business Excellence Awards (2018).

Find out more at www.nalla.co.uk or email her at vicki@nalla.co.uk.

Acknowledgements

First, I'd like to thank my wife, Trang Do, for her patience whilst I wrote this book, but much more importantly for giving me the ambition to see that the book and many of the other amazing things we've achieved together were even possible.

Thank you also to the following.

My parents, David and Michelle Kerr, and my stepdad, Peter Gentry, for always giving me the freedom to make my own decisions, and supporting every decision I've made.

My nan, Rose Bell, for your endless positivity, and for teaching me how to cook a mean roast potato.

Alison Jones and the brilliant team at Practical Inspiration Publishing for your guidance and advice, and for turning this project into a product.

All the contributors who gave their time, insight and candour and became a part of this journey with me. It wouldn't have been the same without you.

Michael Young for developing the Space Tours concept and for the magnificent illustrations that shine throughout this book.

My beta readers, Glenn Wilson, Paul Hulligan and Gina and Mark Smith, for pointing out the flaws in my early draft.

The managers and colleagues I've worked with over the years who helped me to learn my craft. I could name many people here, but to keep it short: Julie White, Mark Chambers and Chris Charlton.

Glenn Wilson again, for being the first person to ask me what it's like to be your own boss.

Finally, thank you to everyone out there who has taken a risk and started a business that solves meaningful problems. The world needs more of you in the years ahead.

Acknowledgements

First, I'd like to thank my wife, Trang Do, for her patience whilst I wrote this book, but much more importantly for giving me the ambition to see that the book and many of the other amazing things we've achieved together were even possible.

Thank you also to the following.

My parents, David and Michelle Kerr, and my stepdad, Peter Gentry, for always giving me the freedom to make my own decisions, and supporting every decision I've made.

My nan, Rose Bell, for your endless positivity, and for teaching me how to cook a mean roast potato.

Alison Jones and the brilliant team at Practical Inspiration Publishing for your guidance and advice, and for turning this project into a product.

All the contributors who gave their time, insight and candour and became a part of this journey with me. It wouldn't have been the same without you.

Michael Young for developing the Space Tours concept and for the magnificent illustrations that shine throughout this book.

My beta readers, Glenn Wilson, Paul Hulligan and Gina and Mark Smith, for pointing out the flaws in my early draft.

The managers and colleagues I've worked with over the years who helped me to learn my craft. I could name many people here, but to keep it short: Julie White, Mark Chambers and Chris Charlton.

Glenn Wilson again, for being the first person to ask me what it's like to be your own boss.

Finally, thank you to everyone out there who has taken a risk and started a business that solves meaningful problems. The world needs more of you in the years ahead.